D0443707

THE **Healthy** **JUICER'S** Bible

THE **Healthy** **JUICER'S** Bible

Lose Weight, Detoxify, Fight Disease, and Live Long

Farnoosh Brock

Skyhorse Publishing

Copyright © 2013 by Farnoosh Brock
All Rights Reserved. No part of this book may be reproduced in any manner without the express written consent of the publisher, except in the case of brief excerpts in critical reviews or articles. All inquiries should be addressed to Skyhorse Publishing, 307 West 36th Street, 11th Floor, New York, NY 10018.

Skyhorse Publishing books may be purchased in bulk at special discounts for sales promotion, corporate gifts, fund-raising, or educational purposes. Special editions can also be created to specifications. For details, contact the Special Sales Department, Skyhorse Publishing, 307 West 36th Street, 11th Floor, New York, NY 10018 or info@skyhorsepublishing.com.

Skyhorse® and Skyhorse Publishing® are registered trademarks of Skyhorse Publishing, Inc.®, a Delaware corporation.

Visit our website at www.skyhorsepublishing.com.

10 9 8 7 6 5 4 3 2

Library of Congress Cataloging-in-Publication Data is available on file.
ISBN: 978-1-62087-403-5

Printed in China

All photographs courtesy of Thinkstock.com

This book is not meant to be used to diagnose or treat any medical condition. For diagnosis or treatment of any medical problem, consult your own physician. Consult with your doctor before beginning any new diet or exercise regimen.

For more information about juicing, please visit www.prolificjuicing.com/healthyjuicers.

To all who seek health and healing from Mother Nature.

Table of Contents

THE **Healthy** **JUICER'S** Bible

Acknowledgments

I want you to start juicing. That's why I wrote this book. I want you to know about this natural healing medicine that is accessible, available and life-changing. I feel fortunate that so many wonderful friends, family and fellow juice lovers gave me a kind helping hand in the writing of this book. First, I want to thank my husband and business partner, Andy Brock, for keeping me on task, for helping me come up with the best outline and layout and for going on a short juice fast with me just to get my final recipes right! I want to give heaps of gratitude to Sandi Amorim of Deva Coaching for sharing her special pulp recipes and being a featured story in Juicer in the Spotlight. I want to thank the owner of Crema Coffee of Cary, North Carolina, Regina Hopkins, for sharing her delicious pulp recipes. I want to thank Israel Torres for his insights on long-term juice fasting, reference on Wolfram Alpha search engine, as well as for being a huge inspiration and a featured story in Juicer in the Spotlight. The other juicing enthusiasts in Juicer in the Spotlight that I want to thank are Marla Trevino, Dan Hayes, Tess Marshall, Shari Romanski, Sarah Cornsnake, Sue Mitchell and Rick Sidley. Their real life stories and experiences with juicing gives you an idea of just how much transformation and healing can happen as a result of juicing. Our humble mission is that you will experience it all for yourself. May this book help you find your way back to total health and harmony with your body. Juice on and prosper!

Introduction

Let food be thy medicine and medicine thy food.
~ Hippocrates

One early summer morning in 2007, America's fitness hero, the late Jack Lalanne, opened me up to the incredible world of juicing, a habit and a lifestyle that has changed my life! Something about the way he described this most natural approach to health connected with me instantly. I believe it was more than a coincidence, just like it's more than a coincidence that you have picked up this book at this point to learn about juicing.

Good things come into our lives at exactly the right time and precisely when we need them. All we have to do is listen and be open to learn and explore. I hope you do that for yourself with this book because I have a lot to tell you about juicing and how it can change not just your health but also your approach to healthy habits and similar changes in your life.

When juicing came to my life in 2007, my health and self-esteem were at an all-time low. I was trying in vain to lose this extra weight I had gained in my stressful corporate job at the time, but the weight itself is never the real problem, of course. The real problem is how it makes you *feel*: unattractive, undesirable, unworthy, fat and, gasp, ugly. And how we feel is the best guidance for what we need to do, and for me, it was time to take massive action.

The usual stuff was just not working anymore—the trips to the local gym, the variations of diets and eating styles and even the physical trainer that was helping me get me in shape. I was working out harder than ever but my body held on to this extra weight all the same. Something else had to intervene. Something I had never tried before. I wanted it to be a natural and fun and exciting change and that morning, I just knew juicing was the answer.

Before long, I had a masticating juicer and I was shopping for fruits and vegetables to juice, and I'll tell you, I was a little nervous. Even if I had been familiar with produce all my life, and grew up eating lots of them in Iran where fruits play a big part of the "health" culture, this juicing business required putting a vegetable through the chute of a machine called a juicer, extracting its fiber and pulp in the process and drinking what's left, the liquid juice. This was a totally different game than eating the whole fruit or vegetable and it scared me a wee bit. But curiosity had overtaken fear and hesitation and I was ready to embrace this juicing business, come what may.

My approach looked something like this. First, I juiced *only* fruits. I call this the safe and familiar route. Orange juice. Grapefruit juice. Orange and grapefruit juice. Apple juice. Apple and orange juice. Apple, orange and grapefruit juice. It was two weeks before I threw some celery and parsley into the mix to make a real green juice.

And here's the shock factor: It tastes great! I am still amazed at how delicious, hydrating, flavorful and appetizing a glass of juice can taste, with the right combination of fruits and vegetables. This has also become one of my golden rules: You should never drink a glass of juice that does not taste good. I will never advocate holding your nose and "chugging it down". Ever. There is no fun in that and juicing is heaps of fun—and this stuff is delicious.

After the fruits, I worked up the courage to juice carrots . . . just carrots at first. When carrot and apple juice tasted more delicious than anything my mind could prepare me for, I was ready to take things to the next level but slowly and with caution. My fears had

resurfaced: What if I made something that didn't taste good? (I did many times and I still lived through it and learned a lot.) Would it ruin my juicing experience? (Ummm, no.) Would I need to return the juicer? (Nope, but I did break it a few times and they fixed it and sent it back—not the end of the world.) Heck, can I even return it? (Yes you can but you won't want to, not after learning how to juice like a pro, baby!)

So I pressed on. Juicing had turned out to be so much fun even for the non-cooking, non-baking me. Curiosity pulled me along and my taste buds were singing all the way, so why resist? By the end of my first month of juicing, I was doing advance recipes like carrots and beets *with* the tops—the green leafy stuff attached to the tops of the beets and carrots in the ground—ginger and garlic, a variety of dark leafy vegetables like Swiss Chard, spinach, kale and a fruit or two to sweeten the whole deal. The juice colors alone would scare my husband and other onlookers out of the kitchen and maybe even out of the house—but if they only knew what they were missing. If they only understood how potent this is, if only they could taste how delicious this is, I thought to myself as I gulped down my green delicious concoction. Yum!

Pretty soon, I could not walk into the produce section of any grocery store without dreaming about juicing everything in sight. I wanted to find out how these vegetables would taste if I put them through the juicer's chute! I wanted to learn how I could best mix and match new combinations to create irresistible juices! For the next year, I experimented with juicing like a

mad scientist on the verge of a new discovery. It was fun, it was exciting, it was exhausting, but more than anything, it saved my health.

First, my stubborn weight came off. Then the extra layer below that, which I had not dared dream of shedding, melted away. Altogether, I lost 20 pounds and for a small person like me, that's a lot of pounds. I wish I could tell you the weight loss was the best part of juicing. Not so. The best part was trading in that sluggish digestive system for a super efficient one, getting the glow back in my skin and the sparkle back in my eyes. I felt like a million bucks and I was happy with myself again.

That's my juicing story in a nutshell. The best part came when I got involved in helping others like you get started into their juicing journey. Now we get into the nuts and bolts of it and prepare you for your own transformation. As you go through this book, I encourage you to get curious and give yourself permission to have fun, to explore new grounds and to discover more about yourself along the way. And please don't get overwhelmed. Think of your juicing journey as a joyful stroll in the park that unfolds at a beautiful pace, not a sprint down the runner's lane that will be over fast and furiously. You will go further and benefit deeper if you take your time and go at your own perfect pace.

Juices of fruits and vegetables are pure gifts from Mother Nature and the most natural way to heal your body and make yourself whole again. You are returning home by going back to the basics.

You are coming back into harmony with yourself. You are starting an exciting journey with a fresh perspective. Let's do that now together.

THE HEALTHY JUICER'S BIBLE

Why Juice? Irresistible Benefits and Your Own Reasons

The obvious reason that you want to learn about juicing is the enormous health benefits, but I warn you, once you learn to make your own sinfully delicious mean glass of green juice, you may come back again and again just for the taste, baby!

You can get excellent nutrition from raw fruits and raw vegetables. Most fruits, despite all their vitamins and nutrients, contain a lot of fructose, the technical term for the fruit's natural sugar. Because of this, it is best to have fruits (with the exceptions of lemons and limes which have nearly zero fructose) in moderation, especially if you are overweight or have high blood pressure, or diabetes or bad cholesterol.

Vegetables, on the other hand, are extremely low in sugar and calories and high in nutrients. In their raw and fresh form, they give you excellent nutrition, but you can only eat so much raw vegetables—the calories are not the problem, but you can give yourself a bad stomachache from all the fiber. Plus, raw vegetables require a lot of chewing especially the harder ones such as carrots, cauliflower, broccoli and celery, and your mouth has to work really hard to break them down properly.

That brings us to one of the most attractive benefits of juicing. You can consume generous portions of fruits and vegetables quickly, without all the fiber. Almost all health authorities and experts recommend we get six to eight servings of fruits and vegetables a day. How often do you get your required dosage, not to mention the variety to hit all your nutrients and minerals? Juicing helps you reach and even go beyond your necessary daily target! Juicing isn't a complete meal by itself so much as a potent supplement to your existing diet.

As you know, juicing removes all the fiber. One of the most common questions from new juicing enthusiasts is if fiber is bad for you: the answer is no. Fiber is very good for you and necessary to a healthy diet, but you cannot consume all the nutrients and vitamins and minerals in the juice without putting your digestive system through a marathon. As a good family friend once put it, you have the issue of dealing with "tonnage." Juicing is the best shortcut to getting tons of nutrients fast and efficiently. Your body immediately absorbs the juice, assuming there is little to no pulp in the juice, and you can get your allotted portion of vegetables and fruits with all the variety that would be otherwise nearly impossible to incorporate into a day's diet.

That's the number one benefit of juicing, but let's talk about all the other irresistible benefits and help you find your own big reason for embarking on this juicing journey.

You Need a Big *Why* to Say Yes to Juicing

> *It is health that is real wealth and not pieces*
> *of gold and silver.*
> ~ Mahatma Gandhi

For the first three years of my marriage, I was on a serious singular mission: to get my husband in shape.

I tried everything to make him lose weight. I bought him diet books, signed him up for gym memberships and hired trainers for him. I cooked him healthy meals and gave him lectures. Boy, did I give him lectures. Every time I thought I had convinced him to see the light, I would be disappointed a week or two later when his motivation—instead of the extra pounds—would melt away and we would back to square one with no change.

You see, I had my strong compelling reasons for him to get in shape, and how can you argue with that? It's a proven fact that being in shape is a necessary element to health and happiness. But those were my reasons, not his. Even though he was 260 pounds at 6 feet tall, seriously overweight and borderline obese, he had no compelling reason to get in shape . . . yet. I am a very persuasive person, but all the powers of persuasion failed, because the truth is you cannot *make* anyone do anything against their own will. This is true for all of us, and it's one of those annoying truths that are best shoved under the rug and ignored. Sigh.

My husband can do whatever he wants when he has found his own reason for doing it. I know that now and I believe that about everyone, including you. So one day, he decided to get in shape for his own reason. Instantly, he changed into a man with a mission. He set out to lose 90 pounds in the course of the following five years. He was more determined and showed more resilience than I had ever seen in him, and sometimes, more than I would have had in me if I were in his shoes. He was unstoppable once he had his own reason to act. That's why he was able to keep going and reach his goals.

Other people's reasons for you to do something, no matter how smart or logical or right they may be, will never be enough for you to do it. You will need to have your own reason for making changes to your health, and in this section, that's what I hope you can do for your juicing journey: Help you find your own big why that makes you say YES to juicing!

So before you embark on this juicing journey, ask yourself:
1. Why am I interested in juicing?
2. What do I want and hope to get out of juicing?
3. What is the biggest motive that drives me to juicing now?

Your answers can be anything, from mild curiosity to weight loss and better health habits. You may want to move towards a more

raw-food friendly diet or you may be interested in getting more nutrients from vegetables into your diet. We talk about all the juicing benefits in the next section, so as you read those, see which one resonates the most with you.

You will notice "Juicer in the Spotlight" stories at the end of every chapter. These are from the fabulous juicing community who graciously shared their stories. I run a virtual juicing clinic at prolificjuicing.com and we have a tight-knit juice-loving community that has grown from it. Everybody has come to the world of juicing for his or her own reasons, and the stronger that reason, the longer they stay with it. You too need to find your own strong reason—*your big why*—for juicing.

With the clinic members, only a few came to juicing because someone recommended they should juice, which got them mildly curious. Then they developed their own reasons to do it, and that's the real reason that keeps them going weeks and months later after the novelty has worn off. Most of the time, a change in their health or their life situation drives them to make a big change and brings them into the natural healing path of juicing. Sometimes, it is the last resort of "getting healthy." Other times, it's curiosity of the hot revolution of juicing, and sometimes, it's the appeal of detox and purification that juicing offers unlike most other diets.

In all cases, they came to it of their own will and desire. Nobody forced them or tricked them into it. They wanted to learn about adding this amazing habit into their life for their own deeply personal reason. You will read their stories as you flip through the chapters, but for now, focus on your own reason for juicing. You need to find yours!

For me, believe it or not, my health was at a horribly low point in 2007—stress, extra weight, awful skin and a state of near depression from feeling so awful—and I wanted juicing to save it. I can say that it most certainly helped, and the more I did it, the better results I got so I kept going. But I also had another reason to start juicing: I just *love* the concept. I am not a cook by any stretch of imagination, but juicing a carrot or a piece of lettuce by pushing it through the chute of my juicer and seeing what comes out gives me excitement every single time. The idea of mixing the fresh juices from these heavenly fruits and vegetables to create delicious concoctions gets me pumped up even five years later.

Juicing is huge *fun* for me. That's the main reason that I juice years later with the same excitement. I see it as an adventure. I am still mixing up new recipes, finding new vegetables, herbs and fruits to juice, and after every adventure, I can hardly wait to share the results with the juicing community to find out their reactions.

Healthy habits do not need to be boring or painful or a turn-off. They can be and should be fun!

Now you need to find your own reason. Knowing that juicing will give you health benefits is not enough of a reason to keep you going when your motivation has taken a hike and you don't "feel like it." Your big why is personal, intimate, yours and only yours, and when you find it, stick with it because you will be able to build a strong juicing habit on top of it.

Maybe you just want a healthy complexion, maybe you want to shed those stubborn pounds or maybe you want to get more vegetables into your diet. Or maybe you just want to have fun with a new addition to your diet. Whatever the reason, make it one that resonates deep with you, one keeps you coming back to your juicer regularly and with excitement!

Think about that as you go into the next section to learn about the irresistible benefits of juicing. Ask yourself: **What is the story that you will be telling yourself and others about why you got into juicing?**

20 Irresistible Benefits of Juicing

Make your own recovery your first priority in life.
~ Robin Norwood

I still remember how I was floating from excitement when I first discovered juicing. It was so drastically different from everything I knew about health and yet so natural. It made perfect common sense, and I could kick myself thinking how it had been accessible to me all these years. Why did I not know about this sooner? How can I best make up for the lost time when I wasn't juicing?

When you can make health choices that get you this excited, you have hit a home run. My excitement came from experiencing one benefit after another about something as simple as juicing fruits and vegetables. Your body may react the exact same way to juicing as mine. You may experience some benefits to a higher degree and some to lower extent. Not all of us will experience every single benefit to its max, but here I list the most notable benefits of juicing with reference sources cited as appropriate. In my years of juicing since 2007, I have experienced all of these to various degrees firsthand, and have seen people in the juicing clinic and community report on similar benefits.

So here are the top 20 irresistible reasons that you should be juicing today, darling. These are not benefits you see overnight, but if you stick to juicing consistently, over time you will reap more of

these benefits. Like a great avalanche that starts small, it will build on itself and surprise and delight you when it gets going.

1. **Absorbs Immediately:** Your body absorbs the nutrients in the juice right away because it does not need to break down food from a solid form. It just absorbs it right into your cells and bloodstream. The delivery of vitamins, minerals and phytochemicals occurs in a form that your body can use right away to feed the cells and nourish the whole body.

2. **Guarantees the Daily Dose:** You can get your full recommended dose of fruits and vegetables efficiently with a juice. It would be hard to have to eat all the vegetables that you need in your diet on a daily basis and you'd consume way too much fiber in the process. With juicing, you get the nutrients without the bulk.

3. **Nourishes Your Body with a Variety of Fruits and Vegetables:** Juicing exposes you to a wide variety of fruits, vegetables and herbs that would otherwise be difficult to integrate into your diet because they may not be your everyday vegetables—fennel, Swiss chard, beet or watercress—and even if you get them, you would need to get creative to work them regularly into your meals. With juicing, you just need to find a recipe that calls for them, or better yet create your own recipe, and just throw them down your juicer's chute!

4. **Detoxes and Cleanses:** Juicing, especially during a consistent basis or as a result of a fast, detoxes, cleanses and purifies your digestive track by expediting the elimination of build-up of waste from the body and giving your digestion a rest. Remember that the number one way your body stays healthy and happy is by being efficient at getting rid of bodily waste on a regular basis.

5. **Creates a Healthy Alkaline State:** Juicing helps your body to return to a healthy alkaline state. The pH balance of human blood needs to stay with a certain range and many foods, especially on the unhealthy side, are extremely acidic, so your body has to work hard to neutralize their effects and return to the desired state. Juicing helps move you in the right direction and closer to your ideal alkaline state.

6. **Makes Your Skin Glow and Your Hair Shine:** Juicing puts the glow back into your skin and the shine back to your hair. Juicing even puts a new spark in your eyes. This benefit may not be immediately noticeable, but if you stick with your juicing habit, darling, you should see a lovely improvement in these areas.

7. **Helps Control Cravings:** Juicing helps you better control your appetite and cravings, especially that sweet tooth we all have! When you drink your greener juices on a regular basis (four to five times a week), you will crave less junk food and start to break those terrible food addictions. The two—juicing and junk foods—cannot co-exist in harmony so you naturally move away from your poor eating habits and gravitate towards healthier choices.

8. **Eases Weight Loss and Maintenance:** Juicing helps you lose weight and maintain your ideal weight, especially with juice fasts. While you should be very careful before going on any length of a juice fast, one of the results of juice fasting is weigh loss. But it doesn't have to be with a juice fast. If you integrate juicing into a healthy diet regularly, you start to shed the extra pounds more naturally.

9. **Raises Your Energy Level:** Juicing increases your energy level. The greener juices invigorate your body, and with all the vitamins and phytonutrients, you will get a burst of energy that, unlike a sugar high with a quick crash, keeps you going for a few hours.

This energy boost from juices is one of the main reasons people enjoy going on juice fasts.

10. **Gives You Mental Clarity:** As juicing helps you clear out the waste from your body, it creates a fresh state of mental clarity. I have experienced this in every juice fast, even ones as short as three days. Juicing eliminates the fogginess and cloudiness from junk foods and other bad foods. The cleaner your internal system gets from consistent juicing, the clearer and sharper your mental state becomes. This helps you focus better at work and on your projects and life goals.

11. **Acts as the Perfect Snack:** Juicing is filling. Instead of snacking on solid foods, you can enjoy a glass of juice. It fills you up, satisfies your hunger, and moves those cravings into the background. It is an excellent way to snack during the day and control your food binges.

12. **Increases Your Immune System:** Juicing boosts your immune system and helps your body resist and fight infections. It also fights the onset of cold and flu if you catch it early and overdose on juice recipes that are high in Vitamin C and antioxidants.

13**. Tastes Irresistibly Delicious:** A glass of juice made with the right combinations can be, quite simply, the most delicious drink you have ever had! Most new juicers are surprised with how delicious juicing can be if you are doing it right. Don't let a bad experience decide the fate of your juicing journey. Make new recipes and find the ones that are delicious to your taste buds.

14. **Generates Mood Balance:** Juicing enhances your mood by balancing your emotional highs and lows. This is a benefit you see over time, say after a month or two of juicing, but not immediately. When your blood sugar normalizes, and you are not putting it through a roller coaster with high-sugar treats or carb-heavy snacks, you have more natural harmony and are less likely to fly off the handle during stress.

15. **Lessens Menstrual Cramps:** This one is for the ladies. Juicing helps with our menstrual period cramps first by helping curb the bad cravings and second with the nutrients found in some specific fruits and vegetables such as pineapple, which is the number one known juice to lessen cramps, as well as beets, celery, fennel, ginger, and leafy greens that contain magnesium. You can make a juice recipe to combine all the goodness in one single glass.

16. **Acts as a Great Hydrator:** Juicing keeps you hydrated. If you don't enjoy drinking your recommended eight glasses or so of water a day, the next best thing is a glass of fresh juice. It is not a replacement for your water, but helps keep you hydrated far better than caffeine and sodas.

17. **Leads to More Healthy Habits:** Juicing introduces you to other healthy habits such as natural healthy foods, self-care, body awareness and even meditation and deep breathing. Juicing

makes you intimately aware of your body and this awareness makes it hard to continue bad habits such as alcohol, drug, and cigarette consumption, among other types of self-sabotage. Juicing helps you get excited about the world of fruits and vegetables. When you have a good habit like juicing, psychologically it would make you think twice about a bad habit that would ruin all the benefits of the good one!

18. **Is Pure Fun:** Juicing is fun. This isn't cooking or baking we are talking about. This is putting fruits and vegetables down your juicer's chute and enjoying a new drink every time. It's exciting. It comes in gorgeous colors. It smells wonderful. It's fresh. It's like a fun lab experiment with tasting after the fact.

19. **Aids the Healing of Physical Ailments:** Juicing has been shown to aid in healing many physical ailments such as joint pain, muscle aches, stomach aches, ulcers and digestive problems. Note that juicing does not necessarily heal the conditions by itself—although there have been cases where people report healing their ailments directly with juicing—but it can expedite the healing process.

20. **Makes You Happy:** That's right. Juicing simply makes you happy. The fresh taste of this hydrating drink makes my cells sing even on a rainy day! I thought I was the only one that felt this way but other juice lovers talk of the same effect. Perhaps you will tell me a similar story after you start your own juicing journey.

These are *just* the top 20 benefits of juicing but by no means *all* the benefits. After you integrate juicing into your life, you will experience even more notable differences that will enrich your health or benefits and will spill over into other areas of your life.

Perhaps juicing will help you start your exercise program or nudge you away from alcohol or inspire you to take up that yoga class.
Perhaps, the mere act of feeling good about yourself and the fact that you are going through such lengths and measures to take good care of your body will give you the motivation to begin to tackle your other health-related challenges and obstacles.

Let juicing be the start of a path toward health and vitality. In yoga, my teacher tells me not to force myself into a pose but to let it happen naturally. If I keep practicing, it will come. I want to tell you to do the same. Focus on your juicing and let it become a natural force that moves you organically in the right direction of healthier living.

So do your juicing. Everything else will start to fall into place as a result.

Weight Loss Versus Health Gain

Just because you're not sick doesn't mean you're healthy.
~ **Author Unknown**

I wanted to include a section dedicated to the popular topic of weight loss to help you think about it in a new light. Our weight—both how we feel about it and how it actually fares in the health chart—is one of the main deciding factors in how we choose our health habits.

The problem with weight loss formulas is that every person's body make-up and composition is different and so the results of each diet vary. The diets are guidelines; they are not an exact science, and following a diet alone does not determine your

weight loss results. If you have experience with this, you know that weight loss is a mental game. You can follow a diet exactly but if you do not *believe* that it will work, don't expect a miracle. Believing comes first.

Your mind plays a key role in this process. Those negative inner dialogues that you have with yourself—like "I'm so fat!", "I need to lose this weight!", "I can't stand being so overweight!", "I hate my body!", "This diet has to work or else!" and similar other disturbing chatter—have a lot to do with how much success you have with those numbers on the scale.

When I first started juicing, I wanted to lose 20 stubborn pounds and boy was I determined. Juicing definitely helped me do that, but it was not only juicing. I had made some shifts in my mental attitude towards health. Juicing can be wonderful for weight loss and you can certainly get great results with juicing regularly—four to five times a week, or better yet, go on a juice fast (see Chapter 10 for details). But what about the times when the weight does not come off even with juicing at this rate?

Sometimes, the harder you try, the less results you get. It becomes frustrating and you get impatient, and you come close to giving up. The evil cycle of weight loss continues and you are back in square one. Sound familiar?

That's where I want you to shift your perspective. When you think in terms of *weight loss*—losing the weight, getting rid of extra weight, dropping the extra pounds and shedding parts of your body that you find undesirable—or any other variations of these words and phrases, you put yourself in a negative and draining state of mind. You put unnecessary pressure on yourself. You add stress and anxiety to your nervous system that then slows down the weight loss—ah, the irony—and it becomes a vicious cycle that you can't escape.

What if you stopped thinking in terms of *weight loss* and instead started to think in terms of *health gain*. Forget the idea of "losing" anything. Let that happen organically. Instead, focus only on *adding* the healthy habit of juicing into your system. Think only about the healthy changes you are integrating *into* your body and not so much about taking anything *away*.

Now, this is a more empowering position in which to put yourself. You are in charge of the *adding,* but you have no control over the *subtracting.* Let the weight loss be a natural result of the changes that you make and think in terms of adding health into your system instead. Juicing is one such addition.

With this mindset, you remove all the pressure you put on yourself, and focus on what really matters, which is the health, not the weight. The weight will gravitate toward its natural harmony for your body. Focus with vigilance on what you can control, in this case, focus on adding the habit of juicing. Start with once or twice a week, and then move up to more. Aim for juicing four to five times a week.

As a result, you will see that your eating desires and cravings will shift, and the juice may start to replace one of your meals—maybe breakfast—followed by a light lunch. Listen to your body and see what else you crave to do as a result of juicing. You may be more interested in a different diet, in more raw foods for instance. That was one of the fun benefits of juicing for me, I got deeply curious in eating more raw foods, mainly raw vegetables that I never before would consider eating because I became familiar with them through juicing.

So focus on the health factors you are gaining on your journey to health and let the weight take care of itself. This is not easy to do especially if you have always focused on "weight loss" as we all have, thanks to our culture. I was obsessed with the scale since the age of 16. I remember weighing myself daily when I was

in college and right after that, when I had more time to focus on exercise and health. My weight determined whether I ate break-fast or lunch that day or more sadly, whether I was kind or cruel to myself. I punished myself constantly if the scale inched up one day, not understanding that those small fluctuations are totally normal. I was young and did not understand how much my mind and my approach to self-care played a role in the weight loss itself. I don't want you to go through that painful experience.

The final desired outcome is to shed the extra pounds and get in good shape; I get that, but how you think about it creates your reality. What if you can create an easy, welcoming and compas-sionate reality such as gaining health, adding healthy habits, incorporating more health and loving yourself along the way no matter what happens? What if you can let go of the stressful and high-pressure expectations you are used to putting on yourself such as losing X number of pounds or fitting into the tiny pair of jeans in the back of your closet?

To help you shift your mindset, use positive affirmations as a prac-tical way to get your thinking in the right place. Affirmations work best when you are already doing the work. Remember, it is im-plied that you are doing the work—eating well, juicing regularly and taking care of yourself. Affirmations are for those times when you want to berate yourself for eating a cookie or not exercising. You still need to stop eating cookies and get to that exercise, but please, can you let go of the punishment and move forward with compassion and love?

Here I have outlined my favorite positive affirmations for health gain versus weight loss. Notice they are all in the present tense, not future. Feel free to modify them and change the words around to make it your own:

1. I am healing my body with excellent self-care.
2. My body now restores itself to its natural healthy state.
3. I only put nutritious food in my mouth to nurture my body.
4. I drink fresh juices to hydrate, cleanse and detox my system.
5. I stay away from junk food because I honor my body and its needs.
6. I forgive myself when I slip up and return to my self-care routine right away.
7. I consume my food with gratitude and without indulgence.
8. I love my body, my temple, my vessel for life, movement, living and breathing.
9. I am healthy, whole and complete.
10. I love and approve of my body and my whole self.

JUICER IN THE SPOTLIGHT

Marla Trevino, who loves the way green juicing makes her feel and continues to return to this singular habit for her overall approach to health and vitality.

"I love green juicing because with juicing, I feel more alive and my energy levels go way up. My sugar cravings subside when I'm juicing. When I don't juice I start craving pro-cessed foods and my food choices are not as healthy. And my complexion feels and looks so much healthier. I've tried eating different ways to see what works best with my body, and I always go back to focusing on green juicing. It's now a must-do in my *feel awesome* toolkit."

Juicing Explained: What Juicing Is and Is Not

First things first. Let's *define* juicing.

What is juicing?

Juicing is when you take a single or a mix of fresh raw fruits and/or vegetables and/or herbs—in any combinations and quantities—and put them through a machine called a juicer. This machine then extracts the pulp—also known as the fiber part—and yields the juice from those fruits and vegetables. You drink the juice part and either discard the pulp or use it in soups, baked good, or broths (check out some of the pulp recipes in this book for ideas).

Juicing refers to these fresh juices that come out of a juicer, yours or someone else's. You need a juicer to do this. There may be sub-standard ways around it like blending the vegetables and then straining the juice out but I won't cover that method in this book. I recommend you invest in a juicer.

What is not juicing?

Juicing is not the same as blending or making smoothies, no matter how much you break down the pulp and liquify the contents. Juicing also does not mean running fruits and veggies through a food processor. If your machine is blending, processing, mixing or mashing the fruits and vegetables, you are surely doing something to them but you are *not* juicing them.

When I talk about juicing in this book, I also mean 100% fresh juice, without any of the fiber. So if you plan on mixing blended fruit and/or vegetables with fresh juice, the result is a delicious smoothie, just not a juice.

Juicing in the context of this book also does not extend to the packaged juices that you can buy at the grocery or health food stores. Those juices are no longer fresh and likely not purely just juice. Sometimes the store makes the juice locally in their juice bar. Some Whole Foods stores offer this so feel free to ask them about it. If that's the case, you have a great health-conscious store to revisit often. Usually you find these types of freshly pressed juices in plastic cups with straw-friendly lids in ice trays in the fresh food section of the store rather than the back refrigerated section.

However, in general, packaged juices go through the pasteurization process, which brings the juice to boil and kills the live enzymes and vitamins, in order to allow the manufacturer to store them properly. This process kills any freshness of your original juice and, what's worse, it changes the taste from what would have been delicious to barely recognizable. Most of the packaged juices may also add chemicals or additives to the contents of the juice. It may still taste sweet and be good but it's not the original taste of those ingredients you are having, it's something else.

In other words, V8, Tropicana and all the more expensive and newer juice brands that are hitting the health food stores do not fall under the type of juicing that we talk about in this book. I had a juicing client once ask me what to do in a pinch. She was traveling and the only accessible option was a store-bought juice. I told her it's probably a net plus choice on the nutrition side, but if it were me, I would go without and just eat whole fruits and vegetables. The taste of packaged juices changes the association in your mind between those fruits and vegetables and their taste, and frankly, I like the true association, which is when you juice them yourself.

A freshly made juice comes directly *and* only from the source of fruits, vegetables and herbs that the recipe calls for. There is no post processing, dilution, blending, pasteurization, long-term packaging and, ideally, no freezing and little to no refrigeration.

Let's now dive deeper into the differences between juices and smoothies, and learn about the four easy categories that you can use as a guideline to classify your juices.

The Difference between Juices and Smoothies

Eat healthily, sleep well, breathe deeply, move harmoniously.
~ **Jean-Pierre Barral**

I love my Vitamix, which is a commercial-grade blender. It has been one of the best investments in our kitchen, but I can't have a conversation about the Vitamix without someone saying, "Oh I love to juice! I use my Vitamix to juice all the time!" No, you don't! The Vitamix is a high-powered blender. It breaks down the tough fruits vegetables and purees them beautifully. It can even turn them into a nice liquid form if you keep blending long enough, but the fiber is still in the final result and you are getting the whole fruit and whole vegetable, just in a more palatable and easier form for your body to digest.

The Vitamix is not a juicer. Neither are any of its cousins, the Blendtec or other brands of blenders but the good news is you can do both: juicing and smoothies.

With juicing, you extract the fiber and drink just the juice. With smoothies, you blend everything. Some people find that juicing is more wasteful, what with all that pulp that comes out. No argument there. Juicing can also get more expensive; it yields less per pound—or kilogram—of fruits and vegetables than a smoothie, naturally, because nothing is lost in the blending process. The other compelling reason that people gravitate towards smoothies is that they like to get the fiber in their diet. All are good reasons for making a delicious smoothie, no argument there. Your Vitamix or a similar powerful blender will break down the fiber considerably, so you are drinking the juice and the pulp and getting the benefits. Plus, smoothies are food—complete foods that can fill you up and keep you happy a few hours, whereas juices get absorbed quicker and are less filling in comparison.

One compelling reason to juice is that enzymes, phytochemicals and vitamins A, C and E—along with minerals like iron, copper, potassium, sodium, iodine and magnesium—are trapped in the indigestible fiber and cannot be assimilated by the body. You get these nutrients in high volume with juicing as opposed to smoothies, and you get them fast!

Your teeth cannot break down the fruit and vegetable to the point where you can extract 100% of the nutrition. Blending helps with that process, sure, but the action of juicing liberates the nutrition from the cellulose in the pulp, and by drinking the juice, you send those nutrients *directly* to the cells of the body, whereas you still have to digest the smoothie in order to do that. With juicing, your body does not have to expend all that energy that it has to use to break down whole foods or even foods in smoothie form. This is especially useful if your body is recovering from an illness and your energy levels are low; you get the nutrition fast without having to work too hard for it!

What surprises me is the polarity between people who juice versus those who make smoothies that they call a "juice." Juicing and smoothies are two different things, period. They can both be fabulous for your health, especially the greener types that call for more vegetables than fruits, such as your green smoothies and green juices. But whoever said you should go into one camp or the other and not both? This is not a religion. You don't have to choose just one! It is just two different forms of consuming your fruits and vegetables, so experiment with both.

I do both but I juice a whole lot more than I blend. Juicing is my first and true love. Juicing is easier and quicker to absorb for my body and I love the hydrating effect of cold freshly-pressed juice, especially after yoga or a long walk. And I love knowing that I get a large amount of fruits, vegetables and herbs into my system by drinking just a glass of juice versus eating or slurping a glass of smoothie. You can also consume more juice than smoothie before you are full, because the first one is a healthy drink and the latter is a complete food.

But smoothies are also great; they can be delicious and they give you a different level of variety to play with fruits and vegetables that may not juice well, such as bananas and avocados and all your frozen fruits. Yum! Smoothies can satisfy you for hours and the fiber is very good for your body.

To help you decide when to juice and when to blend, see the suggestions below:

Blend if:
- You want a filling meal to keep you satisfied for a few hours.
- You are in a hurry and need to do it fast.
- You want the fiber in your fruits and vegetables.
- You want to use some fruits—such as banana and avocado—that do not juice.
- You want to toss in your supplements, seeds, powders and other super foods.
- You have both the appetite and time to consume a smoothie.
- You are more hungry than thirsty.

Juice if:
- You want to quickly absorb the minerals and vitamins in the vegetables and fruits.
- You want to consume a large variety and volume of fruits and vegetables fast.
- You want a flood of nutrition without any of the fiber.
- You want a hydrating drink.
- You want to rest your digestion for a few hours or for longer
- You want to detox and cleanse your system.
- You want a quick energy boost.
- You are more thirsty and dehydrated than hungry.

Like I said, both juicing and blending are great. Juice if it suits your fancy or whip up a smoothie if you are in the mood for one.

Do one, or the other or *both*. Don't get too caught up in the fuss and heated debates about "to juice or to blend." I highly recommend that you experience it for yourself firsthand, and if you can, avoid the chain smoothie shops—they usually just carry fruits. Create your own green smoothie concoction at home, or go to a health food place that makes authentic green smoothies with fresh ingredients.

Incorporate both into your diet if you can. The main downside of doing both is that you would need two separate machines, a juicer and a blender. I've made that investment into my health and don't regret it at all. I hope you make the right decision for you now that you better understand the difference between juicing and blending.

The Three Categories of Juices

No disease that can be treated by diet should be treated with any other means.
~ **Maimonides**

Juicing is like a nice leather chair, you want to *ease* into, not jump on top of it. Ease into your juicing both in terms of what and how much. This is a fun adventure that doesn't get old, but it may get a little overwhelming with all the massive options of what to juice and the world of recipes to choose from. Don't let that happen!

You want to slowly get your body used to the idea of juices and then move to more advanced and potent juices if you are a complete beginner to the whole process. In this section, I show you how to think about juicing in terms of three simple categories. The categories start you out as a beginner and then move you up the ranks. I distinguish between beginner and advanced recipes based on simplicity versus complexity of tastes in fruits and vegetables.

The easiest juices for your body to digest are the ones you have already been drinking in your life, even if in bottled form: the fruit juices. The fruit juices are what your body already knows. You probably have had single fruit juices such as orange juice, apple juice, grapefruit juice, etc. The first step up from that is to mix more than one fruit together to get used to the new taste. Also, now you are making them fresh rather than buying pasteurized juice. Fruit juices are highest in fructose and without the fiber; the high sugar can spike your blood sugar levels if you overdose on them. Limit your fruit juices to half a glass or one glass a day. Also check the recipes section for fruits that are slightly lower in sugar and ways to cut the sugar content on an all-fruit juice by adding lemon or ginger.

As you progress on your juicing journey through these categories, you want to move toward greener juices. The purely green juices are the king of all juices; they are low in sugar and high in nutrients and vitamins. Don't worry if it takes a little time for your taste buds to adjust to the greener juices. These juices have a stronger—and sometimes bitter—taste, and as you move beyond 100 percent fruit juices, you will start to appreciate them and even develop a craving for them. How do you know if you are ready for the more green juices? Well, your taste buds tell you. The more you juice, the more you develop your taste buds for vegetables and herbs that you may have never had. And as you experiment with different recipes, you find out what you like or don't like. Here are two rules that I recommend you follow as you go through this juicing journey:

The first rule: You are the *only* person that decides whether or not you like the taste of a juice. No authority or expert or book should tell you what to like or dislike. Trust your own instincts and taste buds and beware of your preconceived notions. They can trick you and limit your options. For instance, I can't for the life of me get my mom or mom-in-law to try sushi. They have a flawed association in their mind—probably from their upbringing, who knows—that says raw fish is smelly and disgusting and they are terrified of coming in close contact to it, much less eat it! Until they can break that association and approach the experience with a clean mindset, I have no luck sitting down at a sushi restaurant with either of them!

So if you have baseless notions in your head that ginger tastes awful or anything green must be icky, remove them instantly. You don't know that for a fact. Clear your mind of all these unfounded fears and doubts and go into the experience with a clean slate. Tell yourself you are going to find out firsthand, and if you like it, great, and if not, don't worry. Like everything else in life, you can only know for a fact with firsthand experience. Then and only then can you trust your taste buds to tell you the truth and to be the real guide in helping you make the right decisions in your juicing journey.

What if you have had a bad experience, you might ask? This one partly depends on you and how you analyze things. A bad first experience can be a huge turn-off. I get that. But consider what could have gone wrong. Maybe the mix of ingredients that went into that juice wasn't right. Maybe it was too strong. Maybe it did not agree with what you had eaten earlier if you didn't have it on an empty stomach. Maybe you were expecting something else and didn't like the surprise. It could have been a lot of things.

What if you could turn that around? I tell myself to try all good things in life at least *twice*, because if things don't go well the first time, I don't want to miss out on a life-enhancing gift forever. So I give it a second shot for good measure. Can you do that too?

The second rule: It has to be delicious. Period. This is my non-negotiable rule of every glass of juice. Who wants to drink a glass of gross? Not me! I don't care how good something is for me, if it tastes disgusting, like fish oil tablets do (and yes I have tried several brands), then it's not for me. And I would *never* recommend that you down a glass of anything that tastes intolerable just because it's good for you! One of the reasons juicing is so much fun is because it gives you countless—and I do mean, count-less—options. You can create your own recipes to the end of time and tweak them until you get it just right.

You may come across a few juices that taste funny or don't quite agree with you. That's OK. You are allowed to dislike some and love others. Keep trying and take notes on your favorites but don't lower your expectations. Diets sometimes do that to us. It's a conditioning that we have to break. The idea that we have to suffer in order to get healthy is an old adage that has no base in this juicing world—or anywhere for that matter—so discard it please. If you have been wary of trying juicing because you think you might have to trade in your delicious beverages for a scary dark green concoction, you are in for a great treat. It's nothing like that so let true experience guide you, and remember, insist that your green juice be delicious, no matter what!

Now that we have the rules down, here are the three categories of juices to help classify your options:

1. **The Fruit Juices:** These are your easiest and sweetest juices. The fruit juice recipes are 80–100 percent fruit with possibly one or two vegetables thrown in. They may also include optional additions such as raw ginger or turmeric to kick things up a notch. They are your most basic juices, easiest on your digestive system especially if you are new to juicing. They are also the types of recipes to do in moderation due to the high fructose, the natural sugar found in fruits. If you have a sensitivity to sugar, or have a condition such as diabetics where you need to carefully monitor your blood sugar levels, then please check with your doctor about the recipes in this section.

2. **The Fruit and Vegetable Blends:** These are your more intermediate juice recipes in terms of complexity of taste and flavors, as we aim for a more even blend between fruits and vegetables with options to add even more vegetables as you get comfortable. You may start with a 30–70 vegetable to fruit ratio and move up to reverse that to a 70–30 vegetable to fruit ratio in this category. These recipes help you ease into your green juices and develop a taste for vegetables alongside their fruit companions. The fruits in these recipes will cut down any bitterness or strong taste in the green leafy vegetables and still give you lots of benefits from your greens.

3. **The Vegetable Juices:** These are your most advanced juices with the highest potency. They contain 80–100 percent vegetables with optional fruits. The potency factor in these juices is highest and the sugar levels lowest so you don't have to limit yourself on these juices. You can drink to your heart's desire. Beets and carrots are the main two vegetables that have more sugar than the rest but no recipe calls just for those two by themselves. You will need some time to get used to the tastes and find your favorites. This is where you want to make your most regular juices, and where you will get the most benefits from juicing. So this is the ultimate final destination for your juicing journey where you hang out the most and consume the greenest elixirs you can whip up in your juicer!

JUICER IN THE SPOTLIGHT

Dan Hayes, who always had a big aversion to fruits and vegetables, now juices daily and has made it a permanent part of his life.

"I have been an avowed "meat-atarian" my entire life. Never, ever been a veggie guy. I was always fit because of my job and it seemed I could put whatever I wanted into my body and still be able to easily run half-marathons without training or jump out of planes, but then things started creeping up on me: aches, pains, longer recovery after injuries. Deep down I knew I needed to change how I fueled myself. I read a lot of blogs and watched *Fat, Sick and Nearly Dead*. You'll be so motivated to start juicing and you'll want to jump right into it! I'm amazed with how much better I feel getting all those fresh enzymes, nutrients and other good stuff into my body. The changes are awesome. One thing I'm completely confident about is that juicing will be a entirely permanent part of my life."

How to Start Juicing: The Bare Essentials

What do you need at a minimum if you were to start juicing tomorrow? Let's talk about the bare essentials before we add all the bells and whistles and get carried away. You need a juicer. You need the contents of a basic recipe that you can pick up at your local grocery story. You need a small amount of countertop space to make your juice. You need to be near a sink to wash your fruits and vegetables and clean up the juicer after the fact. You *may* need a glass jar with an airtight lid to store it if you make more than one or two servings. Oh and you need a healthy appetite to enjoy your juice!

The one thing that you absolutely need is a juicer. This is the device that properly makes your juice, and in this chapter, I help you choose the best juicer for you based on my extensive research, personal experience and the experience of those in my juicing clinic, as well as interviews with a couple of juicing experts.

Of course, you also need the intangibles. You need a little *time* to prepare, plan and make your juice. You need a little *curiosity* for mixing your fruits and vegetables and tasting your delicious concoction. You need the *willingness* to buy the groceries, follow a recipe and clean up the mess after the fact.

I talk to people about juicing every chance I get, probably a wee bit more than I should but it's just too fun to resist. One of the biggest reservations that people have about juicing is that it is inconvenient and takes a lot of time and effort. They know it has incredible nutritional benefits. They know it's the best thing they could do for their health. They even imagine they would enjoy it, but they have a hang-up about how long it takes and how much it may cost, even if they know that in the long-term, those costs prove to be a fantastic return on investment in their health. Yet they resist!

I agree that juicing is not as quick as throwing together a peanut-butter sandwich or making a smoothie, but it's not as bad as you may think. Those who don't want to do it exaggerate the actual effort and time. There are short-cuts. There are ways to make your workflow efficient and enjoyable and I can help you create a routine that you want to go back to. Plus, juicing comes with other benefits so it's unfair to measure it as a linear experience. It is more than just a simple equation of juicing to get nutrients to your body and being done with it. Juicing permeates into other areas of your life, and like a wonderful perfume, it fills up a whole room, the corridors and the hallways and even the whole house. Think of your body as that house, that temple. Juicing can be transformational to your body and your overall health if you stick with it and approach it with the right mindset and attitude that we cover in this book.

It may take you some time to find your groove into juicing regu-larly. So what? It took me about two years. It's not a race. It's a journey. It's not an overnight success—and really, nothing is. Just come to it with curiosity and willingness instead of the jaded attitude that says: Let's see if this works or not! You may take breaks, you may have lapses and you may go full blast in phases. So remove the pressure you are putting on yourself, approach it with fun and let's go get you ready for juicing now!

How to Select a Juicer That Is Right for You

"Life itself is the proper binge."
~ Julia Child

So by now you know the deal, you Fabulous Juicing Enthusiast: If you really want the full benefits of making and consuming fresh homemade green juices, without short-cuts, you need to invest in a juicer!

How Much Does It Cost?

Remember a juicer is not the same as a blender or a food processor. A juicer is a machine designed specifically to extract the juice part of fruits and vegetables from the pulp. You can find dozens of companies that make juicers these days in all price-ranges costing you anywhere from $50 to one high-end model, the Norwalk, that sells for over $2000. The best investment in my experience of three juicers falls in the $250-$275 range as long as it comes with extended (eight or more years) or lifetime warranty.

But the price is just one factor. You need to keep your budget in mind, but as you determine this one-time investment, think about other hidden costs that you may incur if you go for the cheapest juicer. Here are some other factors that determine which juicer is right for you.

Juicers come in either automatic or manual form. The automatic ones are either a masticating juicer or a centrifugal juicer. The manual juicers are primarily for juicing citrus fruits, so that will not do you any good with your green juice recipes. You want an automatic juicer.

Masticating Versus Centrifugal: Which to Choose?

Now which one to get, a masticating or a centrifugal juicer? As far as heated debates in the juicing community go, we can add this one to the list! People who juice tend to fall into one camp or another. I invested in both types of juicers to test and find out for myself, and I encourage you to do your own research before you decide on your ideal juicer. Here's some information about the main difference between masticating and centrifugal juicers that may help you:

Centrifugal means moving or directed away from a center or axis. A centrifugal juicer is the most common type of juicer you see on the market. They typically have an upright design in which food is pushed into a rapidly spinning mesh chamber with sharp teeth on its floor. It works by spinning at high speeds and during this spinning motion, the vegetables and/or fruits that you have shoved down the chute get grounded to a pulp. The spinning motion forces the juice away from the pulp and pours it into a bowl.

Centrifugal juicers work best with soft and hard fruits and vegetables, but not quite as well with leafy greens like kale or

spinach, and also you cannot juice wheatgrass in a centrifugal juicer. Inexpensive centrifugal juicers can be found for as little as $40 or as much as $500, with most good-quality models ranging in price from $100 to $150. Popular centrifugal juicers include brands like Jack LaLanne's Power Juicer, Breville, Hamilton Beach, Juiceman and L'Equip.

Upside of a centrifugal juicer:

1. It is fast.
2. It has a large chute and you don't need to cut up your fruits and vegetables to small pieces.
3. It is relatively inexpensive compared to its masticating counterparts.

Downside of a centrifugal juicer:

1. It is loud.
2. It wastes some of the juice in the process and produces wet dripping pulp.
3. It yields lower quality juice in terms of taste and texture and is not good for storage. Also the juice is slightly warmer as the spinning tends to raise the temperature and produce a lot of foam in the process.

Masticating means to chew, to grind or to knead into a pulp. Your teeth are an excellent example of mastication in action. Your teeth chew and grind food slowly. After you swallow, the food goes down to your digestive system that, through the process of digestion, begins to extract the juice from the rest of the food. Similarly, a masticating juicer grinds your produce and has no spinning action; it works at very low speeds and yields highest quality juice.

A masticating juicer uses a part called an auger. This auger turns at 80 to 100 RPMs, which is a lot slower than the centrifugal juicers that turn at 10,000 to 15,000 RPMs. This slow auger works like a screw. As it turns, it crushes the fruits and vegetables. It squeezes them against the outside wall of the juicer. The auger motion then forces the juice out one way and the pulp the other way. Since it does this slowly, it does not heat up the juice in the process. This keeps the enzymes and nutrients at a temperature that they can survive. Then you get the benefits of drinking them. Masticating juicers generally have a horizontal design. Because of the slower crushing and squeezing action, masticating juicers can process leafy greens and wheatgrass, and the juice that they produce will last much longer than juice made in a centrifugal juicer, so if you want to store your left-over juice, then a masticating juicer is your best bet. Masticating juicers are pricier than centrifugal models, starting at around $200 and up for most models. Some of the brands to look for are Champion, Omega and Green Star.

Upside of a masticating juicer:

1. It produces highest quality juice and highest amount of juice you can extract from your produce.
2. It is quiet.
3. It does not waste any juice and your pulp is extremely dry.

Downside of a masticating juicer:

1. It has a small chute and you need to take the time to cut up your fruits and vegetables.
2. It is slower and takes longer to juice the same amount.
3. It is generally more expensive.

The Omega's masticating brand juicer was my first juicer in 2007. The main reason I opted for the Omega was its lifetime warranty. It is a great line and has stellar reviews on Amazon but the lifetime warranty pushed me over the edge. If I had to do it all over again, I'd buy this one in a heartbeat.

I have tested the lifetime warranty not once but three times now. The first time was unintentional. Let's just say it is not very wise to cut up your carrot as it is *on its way* down the chute while the machine is running! Never put anything down the augur while the machine is running except the stick that comes with the juicer! The second time was when the motor just stopped running. And the last time was for using the wooden stick from my other juicer, which chipped the augur, and as a result, the machine was stuck and would not come apart. Oh joy! Omega fixed it every time.

My $100 Breville is a centrifugal juicer and mediocre at best in the quality of juice it puts out. The Breville is fast and affordable, but it is the centrifugal model that leaves a lot of juice in the leftover pulp. I have since given it away to a new juicing friend, but I wanted to try it because this was the brand of juicer that many people get started with after Joe Cross made it popular with his film, *Fat, Sick and Nearly Dead*, a must-see for all juicing enthusiasts!

My Greenstar Elite is the newest juicer in which I invested a lofty $560. I would say it works better than my Omega, which cost less than half the price. It yields even more and higher quality juice and dryer pulp than the Omega, but it's hard to justify the sticker price. Still, I love it and use it the most. These days, I alternate between my Omega and my Greenstar.

Israel Torres, a dear friend and member of the juicing clinic, started out with a $50 juicer from Wal-Mart when he started his first 60-day juice fast. He used it consistently for over a month until the motor blew out. Then he invested confidently in a $250 range juicer because juicing had become such a huge part of his life. This is an experience shared by three other juicing members who started with an old cheap juicer under $50. After a few weeks of intensive use, it gave out on them so they invested in a higher-quality juicer for long-term use. If you get a juicer with lifetime warranty, you don't have to worry about having to buy another one so that's something to consider into your budget.

Another factor to consider when choosing the right juicer is the time you want to set aside for juicing. If you are a five-minute, in-and-out kinda person, then a masticating juicer might seem to move at a snails pace. In general, my Breville took about half the time to juice the same amount of fruits and vegetables that the Omega or the Greenstar would take. With the Breville, the whole process may take about 15 minutes, but I have to set aside 25 minutes for my Omega or Greenstar, and note, I gladly do it because I see the value. You may or may not feel that way. Choose what works for you.

With more time, you are also putting in more effort. For example, are you willing to cut up your fruits and vegetables into a size that fits the smaller chute and wait for the slow juicing action of the masticating juicer? If the answer is no and your time is far more valuable than spending it this way, you can make the juicing process a lot faster by investing in the types of juicers that do not require that and come with a larger chute.

Plus you need to think about the complexity or simplicity of the cleaning process post-juicing. I would say the Breville and Omega were very quick to clean, but I spend about five more minutes on cleaning and reassembling the Greenstar.

Here are eight questions to ask yourself before deciding on the ideal juicer for you:

1. Is the juicer easy and straightforward to use?

2. How big or small is it and does it fit your countertop space?

3. Does it come apart easily and are all the pieces dishwasher safe or do they need to be hand washed?

4. Is it easy to quickly assemble the juicer after you wash and dry the parts?

5. What do other buyers say about this in the online reviews?

6. Are there any fruits and vegetables that are a limitation for this machine?

7. What are the parts made of: is it stainless steel or plastic, and how durable is it?

8. What is the warranty and is it possible to get a machine with lifetime warranty at least on parts?

The most important thing about choosing the right juicer is to select one that will *empower* you to integrate juicing as regularly as possible into your life for as long as possible. Knowing yourself and your own priorities, you can decide what aspects of this process might discourage you from doing it again and make sure that you select a juicer that minimizes those aspects while helping you capitalize on the gains. Plus you can always return, exchange and upgrade to a new juicer. The important thing here is to get started juicing.

So do your research, read the customer reviews on websites, look at the prices for the different brands and take everything into account, and then compare it all against what you need and what most matters to you before you buy. Give yourself a deadline though. You can read about product reviews and customer feedback until you are blue in the face—don't! Read enough to do due diligence for your own research, and then make a decision and feel good about it regardless.

A good juicer can last you a number of years and it is the single primary tool you need for your green juicing adventure. After this big decision, you're almost all set for your juicing adventure.

Shopping Tips for Your Juicing Adventures

Tell me what you eat, and I will tell you what you are.
~ G. K. Chesterton

Shopping for your fruits and vegetables is a big part of your juicing adventure. Here, we talk about this fun preparation process: how and where to shop, whether to buy organic or conventional and where to find some of the uncommon vegetables and herbs in your local community.

Planning ahead can be your best friend when it comes to juicing. Get used to planning in advance so you don't go on too many impromptu last-minute shopping trips. Always be planning your day or week's juices and the shopping list that goes along with it. If you can create this process in your schedule, juicing will not get overwhelming. For me, I found it to be relaxing and integral to my life when I planned a little ahead for the week's juicing items rather than running to the store right before I got in the mood to juice. Hey, spontaneity can be fun, and you can enjoy that from time to time—but to make this habit stick, planning can be your best friend.

When it comes to shopping for your produce, remember that the dark leafy vegetables such as kale, collard greens, lettuce, spinach and Swiss chard, among others, have a shorter shelf-life (or fridge-life!) than their denser counterparts such as beets, carrots, apples or peppers. And herbs such as cilantro, parsley, mint and basil have an even shorter fridge-life than the dark leafy vegetables and tend to perish a lot quicker. How you care for them can prolong their freshness a little longer. Also, if you buy them at their freshest state, they will naturally last longer than if you buy them in a more wilted state.

One good tip to help you plan your shopping trips is to buy your herbs and dark leafy vegetables as well as your berries (strawberry, raspberry, blackberry or blueberry) as close to when you will juice them as possible—within three to four days max. You can keep your carrots, beets, turnips, peppers, apples, citrus fruits and other vegetables and fruits of a similar density in the fridge for up to seven to sometimes nine to ten days.

Another thing to keep in mind is that you can juice vegetables up to three to four days past their freshest state and still not notice the lesser freshness factor in your juice as much as you would if you ate them raw and whole. This is why it can be fun to do an "everything in my fridge" juice recipe, which we sometimes do for fun during the juicing clinic. If it's produce that is not in its tip-top fresh state to eat raw, it's just fine for juicing, and you usually end up whipping up a new recipe in the process.

Now where should you shop? Choose a place for produce that is fresh, which is your number one priority, and not overly pricey. This depends greatly on the availability of grocery stores or farmer's markets near where you live. If you've always been shopping

at the same grocery stores, you may not know all the potential shopping stores around you. I did not know about the new health food stores, or the new Indian and Chinese authentic grocery stores as well as the farmer's markets that had popped up around me until I actively searched for them.

With juicing, you will need access to a wide variety of fruits and vegetables, especially if you want to try a lot of different recipes, and you may or may not find all of them under the roof of the same grocery store, so learn about all your options. Go on Google or Yelp and find what is around you; then go on a grocery shopping adventure and scope each of them out to your heart's content.

I have found my Indian grocery stores to be a great place for fresh herbs such as garlic, turmeric, cilantro and parsley as well as fruits such as lemons, limes and tomatoes. I love my general grocery store for the good selection of staple greens such as the spinach, kale and lettuce as well as carrots, beets, apples and all citrus fruits. However, for fresh cranberries that are in season for just a few weeks, or the more hard-to-find plants such as wheat-grass, I may have to make a trip to my Whole Foods store.

Over time, I am impressed with how many more types of fruits and vegetables my general grocery store is carrying compared to 2007 when I first started juicing, but it may be endemic to the growth in the local area where I live. Check your local grocery stores and find out what's available to you and where!

The best way to do your shopping is to first plan out your green juices for the next seven to ten days. Decide what recipes you want to make and then grab the ingredients you need. One idea is to try and make juices with multiple common ingredients in the same week. For instance, make a lot of carrot-based juices or apple-based juices so that you can get those ingredients in bulk for that week and then switch it up with beet-based recipes for the following week.

As for organically grown versus regular vegetables, I would say that you can have a perfectly fine green juicing journey with-out getting anything organic. I have made plenty of juices with regularly grown vegetables. I always wash them well. Soak your

dark leafy vegetables in the sink for five to ten minutes then rinse them thoroughly. Use a vegetable brush for all your root vegetables such as beets, carrots and sweet potatoes and make sure you clean the surface thoroughly before juicing them. With sweet potatoes, I peel them after washing but there is no need to peel beets or carrots. More so than the organic versus non-organic state, what matters most is the *freshness* of the vegetables and fruits. The organic section of grocery stores sometimes has wilted vegetables that are also more expensive. Go for freshness first!

If you wanted to invest in organic produce, choose organic for the types of fruits and vegetables that make the most difference. For vegetables, get your lettuce, spinach, kale, celery and bell peppers organic and for fruits, go for lemon, peach, strawberry, blueberry and tomato if you can find them.

How can you tell if a fruit or vegetable is fresh? Check out these pointers:

1. Dark leafy vegetables start to wilt, get slimy and darker in color or smell bad. Either salvage the remaining good parts or discard.
2. Green peppers tend to slime and get soft and brown in parts; cut out these parts.
3. Cauliflowers get brown specks on them but you can cut out these parts.
4. Broccoli gets yellow and limp; again, you can cut out the bad parts.

5. Lettuce gets very slimy and watery. Discard these leaves.
6. Cucumbers get soft and white spots appear on them. Cut out the bad parts.
7. Cilantro and parsley develop a terrible smell and get brown spots or just become darker and slimy. Discard those stems.
8. Carrots get black or brown spots on them. Cut it out if it has not affected all the parts.
9. Tomatoes get soft brownish spots on the outside and sometimes, black spots in the inside. Cut it out and use the rest.
10. Ginger and garlic will get really soft and puny—as opposed to the nice firmness at their freshest—and develop black spots. Cut out or discard.

When in doubt, just throw it out. I know it's hard to do; it pains me to waste food in even the smallest quantities, but the one rotten vegetable can ruin a big batch of juice and that's even more costly!

Now what can you do to make your vegetables last as long as possible? As soon as you get home, dry them—do not wash them, just dry them—with a paper towel or a regular towel before storage. Most stores in the United States spray water on their vegetables (I wish they would stop doing this!) so when you buy them, they are most likely wet! If you store dripping, wet lettuce in the original grocery plastic bag that you bought it in, you enable the fastest way to spoiling that lettuce! Dry your vegetables completely before refrigerating them. Then use tight lid containers or zip-top plastic bags to store them in and refrigerate them as soon as possible. You can even label them with the purchase date to remember when you bought it and how much time you have before using it.

Some important times to remember:
- Most dark leafy vegetables perish quickly, three to four days on average and five to six days at the most.
- Most fruits and vegetables that need to be peeled last longer, 7-10 days on average, sometimes a little longer.

In general, when a fruit or vegetable is dense, it will hold its ripeness longer. For instance, apples stay ripe longer than say blueberries or blackberries and carrots last longer than lettuce. You should always aim to use your produce at its freshest as quickly as possible. It is a lot of work, but trust me, having that cold freshly pressed homemade juice for your body is wildly worth it when the juice itself is in its most potent and nutritious form. Adding fresh lemon juice also helps the juice keep its freshness and flavor a little longer.

As you may have heard, you should consume your juice as soon as possible after making it, but sometimes you may want to make more and store some. Remember that storing it in a glass container rather than plastic helps preserves the taste. If you have to store your juice, don't keep it for more than 24–36 hours. After that, the potency goes down and the juice becomes "flat." It's still good and delicious but not like when it was first juiced.

If you need to freeze your juice for any reason at all, don't keep it longer than one to two weeks at the most. Freezing your juice is an option if you have a crazy busy lifestyle. I have frozen my juice only once and the defrosting was messy and the juice tasted flat and blah even after a mere 24 hours in the freezer. Freezing seems to remove the yumminess altogether, whereas refrigeration for the same period does not do that. Keep freezing as the last resort.

JUICER IN THE SPOTLIGHT

Tess Marshall, who was afraid of her juicer, is now bold and fearless as she makes and enjoys her regular glass of green juice.

"My family owned a produce farm and our daily diets were filled with fresh fruits and vegetables nine months out of the year. As children we were never sick. I'm familiar with the benefits of a healthy diet. My daughter started preaching to me about juicing about a year ago. I simply wasn't ready until I met Farnoosh at a juice bar in Portland, Oregon in summer of 2012. My juicing began as an investment in my health. My first tall frothy glass was delicious and brought back memories of my childhood. I remember thinking, "It's like I'm drinking a garden! Make a life long commitment to juicing and invest in a good juicer. Make juicing a ritual and do it with an attitude of gratitude."

Let's Talk Ingredients

Getting your ingredients is one of the most fun parts of juicing. You think you know your fruits and vegetables? Think again! Before I started juicing, I thought I was pretty savvy about produce but I knew nothing! I had no idea what a Bok choy or Swiss chard or kale was. I did not know that raw turmeric came in the form of root vegetables but in a bright orange color instead of the light yellow color of ginger, and that watercress and parsley could be so good for me. And I definitely didn't think that I could juice all these fabulous greens in my machine!

Discovering new fruits and vegetables, herbs and plants is the first part of the process. The real learning begins when you discover what goes with what, and what ingredients should never mix together! You can experiment on your own, and to some extent you will, but in this chapter, I will share with you the best guidelines on how to mix and match your beautiful produce to make delicious juices.

If you are apprehensive about trying new things that you have never heard about, I totally understand. You can stay with very basic recipes of fruits and vegetables that you are familiar with and still get great benefits from juicing. But after a while, you may get tired of the same old recipes, and being open to new tastes can enhance your juicing experience. Imagine going to your juicer with an element of surprise about how your juice will taste with a new recipe. Most of our apprehensions are just mental. I used to be against mixing orange into any green juice until I tried a new recipe with orange, carrot, and beet at a local juice bar on my travels. Wowza! Now, orange and carrot are one of my favorite combinations. I created a whole list of new recipes based on an orange-carrot foundation.

An open mind can be a good thing to have when you are juicing! And ask yourself: What's the absolute worst thing that can happen? You don't like the juice? So what? You will have wasted some produce and that's a shame, or a few bucks at a juice bar, but then you will know for certain what you like and don't like, instead of guessing. But, you should follow two rules before you try new ingredients: (1) Look them up in this book or other sources online to make sure it is something that can be juiced and mixed with your set of produce and (2) make a small batch of it to taste before you commit to a whole big jar.

One of my worst juicing experiences came from getting a little too adventurous and not following my own rules. I had just made a huge jar of one of my most favorite green juice recipes, and then, right before finishing it, I decided to make things exciting by throwing one extra ingredient: Radish! I cannot tell you what an odd terrible taste that radish added to my heavenly drink. I was in tears! I could not stand the taste so I had to discard the whole thing. Because I knew the recipe so well, there was no doubt that the radish was the culprit. I have never juiced radishes since then, and you won't find any recipes here with radish as an ingredient. But listen, this is a rare incident in my five years of juicing. I will give you as many guidelines as I have discovered on what goes well with what so you make good safe decisions, and you now know the two simple rules if you want to create a recipe of your own.

The radish story brings up another point. I love eating radishes as whole raw vegetables. I love the taste, the bitterness, and it goes great in a bed of greens, especially with some cheese and crackers. But I did not like radish juice. The opposite is also true. You may not like eating raw whole vegetables or fruits of some kind but you may really enjoy them in juice form, as it mixes with other ingredients and also is much easier to digest. Let those teeth rest from all that chewing!

When you are open to new tastes, you get the most invaluable thing: firsthand experience as to whether you like something or not. Then you can honor that. My rule of thumb is to try everything in life at least twice—although juicing radish isn't getting a second chance so there *can be* exceptions! I say twice because the first time something may not work out for whatever reason. My first experience with yoga was boredom in a YMCA yoga class with hip hop music and a teacher that was more concerned with her own "workout" than what the students were doing. In the second class, I still got bored but my hands reached further as I bent to touch my toes. Wow. I thought I knew my body and that ounce of progress kicked off a decade-plus long yoga path all because I went back for a second class. Give things worth doing in life a second chance!

So with an open mind, ready taste buds, and a curious attitude, let's dive more into the chapter and learn about the darling items of most juice recipes, guidelines on what to juice and what not to juice and respecting your taste buds.

Guidelines on What to Juice and What Not to Juice

The part can never be well unless the whole is well.
~ **Plato**

You can juice just about anything! I love to say that to new enthusiastic juicers who walk on eggshells when it comes to juicing any new fruit and vegetable just to relax them. But there are selections of produce that are off-limits and best not to juice. Some have no juice to offer and are better eaten whole or blended or cooked. Others are bitter and not edible at all and, therefore, certainly not "juiceable."

Here are some guidelines on what you can and cannot juice. I give you my experience as well as research that may or may not suggest otherwise.

The "Unjuice-ables": Here is a list of things that I suggest you *do not juice*, or the unjuiceables, if you will, because of texture, taste, juice density or how poorly they mix with other vegetables and fruits:

Rinds—First, all citrus rinds with the exception of lemon and lime are not juiceable. So always peel your orange and grapefruit. The rind is bitter and can be used instead as flavor enhancer in your cooking or baking if desired but not for the juicer. Second, rinds for all melons such as watermelon, cantaloupe, honeydew, winter melons as well as pineapple are not juiceable. Always peel first before running the fruit through your juicer. Pineapple rind is extremely tough and can damage your juicer.

Banana—Bananas have very little juice and would be a complete waste down your juicer. Eat them whole. Blend them. Bake with them, but no juicing a banana!

Avocado—Same as bananas, even if they may have slightly more juice, never put avocados into your juicer. Blend them, add them to salads and eat them whole instead.

Eggplant—Eggplants are not for the juicer! They just don't have enough juice and taste awful raw and juiced. They also have a dense consistency that really doesn't work very well with your juicer.

Rhubarb—Don't juice rhubarbs either. It does not taste very good and it's very hard on your juicer. Best to avoid.

Coconut—I love coconut raw and coconut juice but don't put the coconut meat through your juicer. It is extremely hard on your juicer and not much juice will come out.

Okra—Okra does not yield much juice; it is a slimy texture that's not good for your juicer. It is best left just for cooking. No juicing okra!

Potatoes—You will find recipes online that call for potato juice. I have only juiced sweet potatoes and they are delicious and full of nutrition but the regular potato has very little nutrition and/or sweetness.

Mushrooms—Leave mushrooms for your soups and cooked foods. There's no juice to be had from mushrooms!

Mustard Greens—These are extremely bitter and strong. You can technically juice them but they are left off the recipes in this book.

Edamame or soybeans—No juicing these. They hardly have any juice and are best eaten cooked with salt!

Onions, leeks—The onion family is generally a "proceed with caution" type. I have juiced leeks before—the bulb and the green leaves; they are extremely powerful and pungent and can jam your juicer. Onions are also powerful—I have only juiced white onions in small quantities in a few recipes.

Squashes—There are many squashes out there. The winter squash is the hardest to juice . . . making it an unjuiceable by our juicing standards in this book! Instead cook with them! Summer squashes are much softer and you can experiment with those if you like. I have never juiced squashes and prefer to eat them instead.

Green beans—Not much juice to be had from green beans and not much flavor, but you can try it.

Here's a list of most fruits and vegetables that you can juice in their raw fresh form. Never juice frozen or thawed fruits or vegetables please! The recipes in this book will call for these ingredients:

Fruits

Apple	Lime	Plum
Blackberry	Kiwi	Pomegranate
Blueberry	Mango	Raspberry
Cantaloupe	Melon	Strawberry
Cranberry	Orange	Tomato
Grape	Peach	Watermelon
Grapefruit	Pear	
Lemon	Pineapple	

Herbs

Basil	Fennel	Parsley
Cilantro	Garlic	Turmeric
Dandelion	Ginger	
Dill	Mint	

Plant

Wheatgrass

Vegetables

Arugula	Carrot	Lettuce
Beets	Cayenne pepper	Onion
Belgian endive	Celery	Parsnip
Bell pepper	Collard greens	Spinach
Bok choy	Cucumber	Sweet potato
Broccoli	Jalapeño pepper	Swiss chard
Cabbage	Kale	Watercress

The Darling Items of Most Juicing Recipes

To eat is a necessity, but to eat intelligently is an art.
~ **La Rochefoucauld**

What are some of the staples of most juicing recipes? If you visit juice bars, you will notice that almost all of them use carrots, apples, beets and oranges as their four most common ingredients. They stick to these four because they are sweet and delicious, they make for a great base, they don't perish quickly, which is something to keep in mind for the logistics of running a juice-bar, and almost everyone likes them. All in all, it is an easy way to introduce the public to the idea of juicing. Then they generally use celery, cucumber and possibly one leafy green such as spinach for their add-on ingredient. Any of the base ingredients—carrot, apple, beet, orange—would yield a delicious combination with these less-sweet greens and with many other greens that they don't even carry.

These foundational fruits and vegetables are some of the darling items of most juicing recipes. It will behoove you to always have one or two of them in your fridge. They are available in just about every grocery store. They don't perish quickly; you have at least a week to ten days to use them, and with them around, you will have a base for just about any juice you want to make.

On top of that, you can have additional darlings in your fridge in the herbs, greens, fruits and other selection categories (see below). If you have at least one item from each of the darling categories below, you can always whip up a delicious juice. It's like a Make-Your-Own menu. In Chapter 9, we will learn how to improve the recipes in this book and create your own, so these guidelines will be handy then. These combinations below will make you a powerfully nutritious and delicious juice every single time, and if you have any additional ingredients, you can experiment with adding those.

Foundational Base Darlings:

These are the darling items for foundational base of your juice:

Carrots: Delicious and sweet and yielding lots of juice, these can be a perfect base for a green juice or they can be mixed with other fruits. No peeling necessary; just wash well and cut off the ends.

Apples: Any kind will do. Get a mix so you have the sweeter kinds such as your Yellow Delicious apples as well as the more sour ones such as the Granny Smith green apples. Apples go in just about every recipe and can cut down the bitterness of your green leafy vegetables. No peeling necessary, but you can cut out the seeds and the stem. I tend to throw my core into the masticating juicer. It knows to discard the seeds, but it's up to you.

Beets: Beets can be a base on their own, but when you are starting out, you may want to use one more base such as carrot, apple or orange to add more sweetness to the juice. If you are getting used to more vegetable-based juices, then a beet alone can be a perfect base. No peeling necessary but wash very well, because beets come from the ground and can be muddy. Then cut off all the black parts and the top head of the beet root.

Tomatoes: Hydrating, sweet, and delicious, tomatoes make a great base and go very well with all vegetables and most fruits. You can use any tomatoes. Roma tomatoes, which are slightly less expensive, are a good choice.

Oranges: Oranges add a citrus flavor, mix really well with carrot as a secondary base and can be perfect for a green juice with the dark leafy vegetables. Oranges go beautifully with beets as a secondary base. Remember to always peel your oranges.

Lemons: Lemons cut the bitterness of any vegetables, add a fresh citrus flavor to the juice and give you heaps of antioxidants. They also help preserve your juice longer, and if you run your lemon through the juicer last, it helps clean out your juicer. No peeling necessary.

Limes: Same properties and goodness as lemons. The flavor of lime is different, so try it in small quantities. It goes well with lemon too as well as with all your base ingredients. Most recipes will call for lemon, but in a pinch, you can use a lime. No peeling necessary.

Nature's "Medicine Cabinet" Darlings:

These three ingredients can turn your glass of green juice into a powerful healing drink. Use them often but start out slowly and in tiny quantities to develop a taste for them first:

Ginger: Raw ginger root is sharp and pungent and will wake you right up. You can start with a thumb-sized piece and increase over time, and you can add it to just about any recipe. No peeling necessary; just cut out any dark spots with a knife. You can find this in most grocery stores and it stays fresh for a week to ten days in your fridge.

Garlic: Raw garlic can enhance the aroma and flavor of your juice. Start with 1 single clove and work up to 2-3 cloves. This stuff is strong and pungent but oh so good for you. Peeling is necessary and throw it in first so the rest of your ingredients clean out the aroma from the juicer.

Turmeric: Raw turmeric may be hard to find so look for it in specialty health stores or Indian grocery stores. It looks just like ginger root but it's a bright orange. It is rather sweet and delicious with a hint of sharpness. Start with a pinkie-sized piece and go from there. This may make your juicer yellow so you need to wash it right away after juicing. No peeling necessary. Throw it in first so the other vegetables can lessen the coloring.

Dark Leafy and Non-Leafy Green Darlings:

The darling items from the green leafy vegetables selection:

Spinach: Spinach is the king of all dark leafy vegetables. It is also the least bitter and most tolerable one when you first start juicing. Be sure to wash your spinach thoroughly and use it quickly— it has a very short shelf-life, so carefully look for any wilted dark leaves to discard before juicing it. Spinach is notorious about looking good on the outside with wilted leaves when you spread out the bunch, so take a good look first.

Kale: Kale has become one of my most favorite dark leafies. It is dense and makes a rich green juice recipe. It works great in the absence of spinach or in combination with it. It is available in most stores and in different kinds—all are juice-able. Kale lasts longer than spinach in the fridge. Look for the rare yellowing parts and cut them out before you use them.

The darling items from the non-leafy green vegetables selection:

Celery: Celery has a very distinctive non-sweet taste but it goes great with your bases, lasts a while in the fridge, is available in just about every store and mixes well in most recipes. Just cut out the end of the stems before juicing. If you like the taste, it can be good to keep it around.

Cucumber: Cucumbers are hydrating and add a delicious flavor to your juices. You can juice all kinds of cucumbers; my favorites are the long Italian cucumbers. No peeling necessary.

Herb Darlings:

The darling items from the herbs selection:

Parsley: Parsley is one of my favorite herbs to juice. It adds a great flavor and aroma to your juices, but you need to use it within three to five days of purchase. Make sure it is fresh. Take out the yellow parts.

Cilantro: Another great herb to have around. The leaves of cilantro are thinner than parsley so it perishes more quickly, but just like parsley, it adds great aroma and flavor to every green juice. People either hate or love the taste of cilantro. If you don't care for it, use parsley.

Fruit Darlings:

The darling items from the fruits selection:

Pineapple: If you have access to pineapple and are willing to cut it up and peel it completely—including the hard middle part— then you can add a few pieces to your dark green juices. Because pineapple taste is delicious and overpowering, go easy on how much so it doesn't dominate the taste.

Pear: Pears can be a great replacement for apples and go very well with most green juice recipes. They have a beautiful sweetness and a rich flavor that cuts down any bitterness, and they mix very well with the dark leafy vegetables. No peeling necessary but cut out the seeds and the stem. Most stores carry them. I use the green pears but you can juice every kind of pear.

JUICER IN THE SPOTLIGHT

Shari Romanski, who has been able to lose stubborn weight with juicing and sleep better and even say good-bye to junk food.

"There is so much talk about what is healthy and a gazillion different programs that will 'fix' you, but I love the overall simplicity of green juicing. What I've noticed since consistently juicing is I do not crave junk food. I've always enjoyed fried, salty and sugary foods. I love it when I have something in mind that I buy to get it out of my head and after I start eating it, I don't enjoy it like I used to. Green juice has grown on me over time and I now love it, so I'd rather add in extra fruit if I want something sweet versus a piece of cake! A second change is that I sleep through the night. In the past I had a hard time shutting down my mind, and when I did fall asleep I would wake up at different times through the night. Now I can sleep through and wake up refreshed. I look at juicing as a good drug of choice."

In the Kitchen: Getting Ready to Juice

All the preparation and the talk have brought us here into the kitchen for the actual experience now. I bet you are raring to go, ready to get started and to make your own fresh delicious juice!

By now, you have selected and maybe even bought your juicer, which is the biggest decision in juicing. Once you have your juicer, you can start getting excited about all the other fun preparations you get to do in your kitchen. In this chapter, I want to help you think about building a fail-proof efficient system for your juicing and here's why:

- A good system will make your juicing activity seem more like a routine and a habit to which you often want to return.
- A good system will keep you juicing longer because it allows you to go onto autopilot when you don't feel like juicing.
- A good system will help you stay motivated, because if you can be efficient and organized about your juicing, you will enjoy it more.

The system will include a preparation phase, which will talk about the art of storing and cleaning your vegetables, and a setting up phase for the juicer, which includes washing, peeling (if need be) and cutting the ingredients that the recipe calls for. I remember having to do all of this in my old tiny kitchen before I had a system. I made a giant mess every time I juiced and felt that the whole process was too big and unstructured for me. Then I developed a system, and even my small counter-space seemed more than enough to accommodate my then-daily juicing craze!

I also want to give you a quick walk-through of the whole process because it really isn't as bad as you think. I know I can't be there with you in your kitchen to help you, and if you could just see my enthusiasm for juicing, you'd not be surprised that I want to help every single person get going. Alas, I can't be with you in person, so I wanted to do the next best thing and talk you through it in in this chapter. These are the things that I wished someone had spelled out for me, all the subtle stuff that you are supposed to somehow know, like what goes in the juicer first and what to do when the juicer gets too full or blocked up and why does the juicer create all that foam! We are going to cover it all in detail, baby!

A good, fail-proof and efficient system combined with top organization is your best friend as you enter the juicing world, so keep that in mind as we enter your kitchen and get ready for some fun.

Getting Organized: Cleaning and Storing Your Produce

If you can organize your kitchen, you can organize your life.
~ Louis Parrish

You've just come home from a long and full shopping trip to one or more grocery stores. You're carrying large brown paper bags filled to the brim with the best selection you could find—fresh fruits, vegetables and herbs. You put everything down on the kitchen counter and . . . Quick, what's the next thing you need to do?

I am probably not the only person who would then jam all her produce into the fridge only to sigh in frustration just 48 hours later when my greens had started to wilt and rot in the wet dripping plastic bag from the store. In the US, and perhaps other parts of the world, grocery stores spray water on the produce constantly to keep them fresh. But this becomes a problem for the dark leafy vegetables when you purchase them in that wet state. The high exposure to moisture in a plastic bag makes them rot quickly if you don't do something about it when you come home.

Here are some suggestions to take care of your produce right after you get home:

1. Put all your produce on the counter first.
2. Store all the fruits and root vegetables like carrots and beets in the fridge. Pat dry your celery and cucumber then store in the fridge.
3. Lay out your leafy vegetables—lettuce, spinach, cilantro, parsley, kale, Swiss chard, watercress, basil and the like—on either paper towel or a dedicated kitchen towel and then pat them dry as much as possible. Let them sit on the countertop for no more than 20 minutes as you do this.
4. As you dry them, if you notice yellow or brown or wilted leaves, discard them.
5. After you have dried them as much as possible, store them. Choose either large zip-top plastic bags or plastic containers with tight lids. With the zip-top plastic bags, make sure you let all the air out before you zip it up.
6. Store each vegetable in a separate bag and label your zip-top bags with a pen or a label maker. Put the name of the vegetable and the purchase date.
7. Put all your produce in the fridge. Throw away the web plastic bags in which you bought them. All done!

This whole process should take you no more than 30 minutes to do for two full brown paper bags of produce! It gets easier and faster as you do it more and more, and if you do this every single time, your produce will last so much longer, not to mention how organized you will be. Imagine if everything is properly cleaned and labeled in the fridge. You can grab what you need in seconds and put the leftovers back in the proper containers for later.

Remember: Do not wash any of your vegetables until you are ready to use them. Washing produce before storing may promote bacterial growth and speed up spoilage, so it is often recommended to wait and wash fruits and vegetables just before use. Also, you will need to wash your produce thoroughly whether it's organic or not. The number of pesticides used in the soil may be less in the organic produce, but they have still traveled a long time and have been handled by numerous people and in various storage boxes. Washing them thoroughly is critical.

And remember to remove the stickers on your produce. They can clog up your juicer and be a mess to clean up later. Just cut them out after washing and carry on with your juicing.

When you are ready to use your produce for juicing, here are some guidelines on how to properly clean them:

Leafy green vegetables. Separate and individually rinse the leaves of lettuce and other greens, discarding the outer leaves if they are torn and bruised. Leaves can be notorious to clean at times so immersing the leaves in a bowl of cold water for a few minutes helps loosen any sand and dirt. After washing, blot dry with paper towels or use a salad spinner to remove any excess moisture.

Apples, cucumbers and other firm produce. Wash well or peel to remove waxy preservative. I do not peel these because they contain nutrients but you may choose to peel waxy cucumbers.

*Citrus fruits—lemons, limes, oranges, and grapefruits—*Just rinse them well under lukewarm water. You can use a vegetable brush on the surface of orange and grapefruit if you like before peeling them for your juicer. Lemons and limes don't need any peeling.

Root vegetables. Peel just the bottoms of your carrots, beets and other root vegetables and clean them well with a firm scrub brush under lukewarm running water before cutting them for the juicer.

Melons. The rough, netted surfaces of some types of melon provide an excellent environment for microorganisms that can be transferred to the interior surfaces during cutting, so make sure to clean the surface well. Just use a vegetable brush and wash melons thoroughly under running water before peeling or slicing.

Hot peppers. When washing hot peppers, wear gloves and keep hands away from eyes and face!

Peaches, plums, strawberries and other soft fruits. Wash under running water, be gentle with them and dry with a paper towel.

Grapes, cherries and berries. Store unwashed until ready to use but separate and discard spoiled or moldy fruit before storing to prevent the spread of spoilage organisms. Wash gently under cool running water right before use.

Herbs. Rinse by dipping and swishing in a bowl of cool water and dry with paper towels. The leaves of cilantro and parsley and basil and the like are tender so be gentle.

With these guidelines, you should become an expert at washing your produce thoroughly and have the cleanest fruits and vegetables ready for your juicing adventure.

One last thing about the cleaning and organizing and washing process is to have fun with it. Turn up some music. Listen to your favorite podcast or start an audio book. I remember listening to my French podcasts when I had first started juicing in 2007. It was something fun to do and it made juicing more exciting. You may have to turn up the audio volume when the juicer gets going but in the before and after parts, there is a lot of prep time and there's nothing that says you can't multitask! If you work hard to make this whole process a fun routine, you will not only get good at it, you will look forward to it. It can become your zen escape from the crazy rushed world that you live in the other hours of the day, and taking care of your raw fresh fruits and vegetables can be a great way to ground yourself, to quiet your mind and to remind yourself that you are doing this to nurture and nourish your body. What a beautiful thought and a worthwhile use of your time and effort.

A Total Walk-Through: Not As Bad As You Think

Clogged with yesterday's excess, the body drags
the mind down with it.
~ Horace

I have read a lot of books and blogs on juicing and I don't recall a single one that covered guidelines on specifically how to get set-up and go. Maybe they assumed that you know what you are doing or that you could just Google it or read your manual to fill in any gaps. Well, when I was first getting started, I could have used all the nitty gritty details that I am about to share with you here, so may you find it useful as a brand new juicing enthusiast.

Let's do a total walk-through because spelling it out always eases any tension and unease that we may have about things. Note that this walk-through is for a masticating juicer but it's a very similar process for any type of juicer.

First things first, get your juicer out and, better yet, find a permanent or semi-permanent place on the kitchen counter for it. Studies have shown that if it is out of sight, you will likely not use it. I have had readers tell me that they forgot they had a nearly brand new juicer because they put it away in a cabinet after one use! Even as a frequent juicer, those few times when I have needed my countertop space for other things and have cleared my juicer out, I have forgotten to juice as frequently until I set the machine in its permanent space again. So make some permanent room on your countertop space in the kitchen, near an electric outlet where you can easily plug and unplug your juicer and preferably very close to the kitchen sink. I know that's prime real estate so do your best. You don't have to keep all the containers that come with your juicer on the counter, just the machine itself. Your goal is to integrate this juicer into your kitchen and countertop space as seamlessly as possible so help it belong to the kitchen just like any other favorite appliance!

Now, after you establish the right home for your juicer, you need to feel comfortable *using* it—this includes assembling it together quickly and efficiently, knowing how small to cut your produce for your chute, managing the pulp and the juice that comes out, pouring out your juice in the right containers and taking your juicer apart to wash, clean, dry and reassemble it after the fact. I know this sounds like a lot but trust me, anything else that you do well would seem this comprehensive too if you were to outline it step by step.

With my Omega juicer, it used to take me about ten minutes just to reassemble it until I learned the shortcut to getting the auger right into place. After that, it was a 30-second job! My husband would hand me the parts because he didn't want to deal with it and bam, I'd put it back together and set it up for its next use in seconds. With my Greenstar, the twin-gear technology is a wee bit more complicated so it takes me about a minute to reassemble all the parts. With my old Breville, it was also just a matter of seconds. Once you learn your machine inside out, it becomes second nature.

All right, so let's continue with our walk-through. You have your juicer ready to go. You just need to take out the right containers for juice and pulp and set them out. You have your recipe and know what you need and how much. You have your produce on your counter. The next task is to wash your fruits and vegetables thoroughly, and pat them dry—they don't need to be completely dry since they are going into the juicer—and put them on your cutting board to cut into the appropriate size that fits your machine's chute.

If any of your fruits and vegetables need peeling, now is the time to do that, too. Most masticating juicers have a relatively small chute. To make your cutting easy and seamless, use a big sharp knife, it is easier and faster. If you are not very good with knives, go on YouTube and search for a knife-using lesson 101 to pick up some quick skills. This can save you a lot of time over the long haul. Oh, and invest in a good cutting board and a sharp knife. You'll be using them a lot.

After you lay out all your vegetables and fruits on your cutting board, I recommend snapping a quick picture. It's the best way to remember exactly how much of what you made, and you can document your juicing journey through photos. This comes in super handy if you feel lazy for writing it all out in your juicing journal—more on that later.

Then it's time to put these puppies through the chute and juice them. This is the most exciting part of the juicing process for me, almost as exciting as drinking the delicious mix afterwards. Here's the best way to go about it: If you are juicing dark leafy vegetables, put those through your juicer first. You can roll up the leaves and gently slide them down the chute and let the auger pull them in. This works best for the vegetables with long thin stems and saves you the trouble of pushing them down. Follow with any hard vegetables such as carrots, beets and cucumbers. Then do your ginger, garlic, turmeric. Save your fruit for last and put your lemons and limes at the very end so they can clean out the juicer as they go through.

If your juicer gets a little blocked during the process—and this can happen to the best of juicers, so don't panic—you probably put things in a little fast so slow down. This is where the expression "slow down to speed up" makes a lot of sense. Pacing things will save you time later! Make sure to push down everything, and if anything gets stuck down the chute, and you can't get it out with the proper utensils made for pushing down the chute, then stop the machine and see if you can remove the stuck fruit or vegetable after the machine is turned off. Never, *ever* stick your knife down the chute at any time but especially if the machine is running. You can cut the auger and the blade and hurt yourself! Over time, you will learn the pace of your machine and the size of your chute so you can cut up your vegetables and fruits just right!

If your machine produces too much foam, just use a strainer or remove it from the juice surface with a spoon after you finish juicing. You can of course drink all the foam but you may not want all that foam in your juice. This is totally a matter of personal preference. Using a good quality juicer will cause the least amount of juice foam. My Breville produced about twice as much foam as my masticating juicer for the same exact recipes. Part of the reason was because the centrifugal machine pushes out the juice with such force that the motion itself generates a lot of foam, so the foam in the centrifugal machine is much more air-filled than the denser foam in its masticating counterpart.

Foam is indicative of oxidation of the juice and it is believed that it lowers the antioxidant benefit. Less foam then yields more antioxidants to your body but hey, the foam can also be tasty, especially from apples, pineapples and strawberries. I spoon those right into my mouth but only from my masticating juicers. Just sayin'!

In addition to the foam, if you don't use a strainer you may get more pulp in your juice than you desire. If you are fasting, then you want to minimize if not completely remove all extra pulp in your juice because it will activate your digestive system, which should be at rest during a fast. Some juicers, such as the Greenstar Elite, come with variable size screens for the juice outlet—one very fine and one coarse. I have used both and enjoy the higher pulp in the juice for my fruit recipes and the cleaner more

pure juice in the green juice recipes. If you have that option on your juicer, play with that.

The Omega uses plastic containers for catching the juice and the pulp, and by the end of three months use, these containers had changed from a clear color to a permanent yellowish brown color. For the Greenstar, I love that they provided glass containers. If you can, pour your juice out into a glass container regardless of the container your juicer comes with. This way your juice won't pick up any of the plastic smell and the glass will wash so much easier!

After you finish juicing and before you move into the cleanup stage, start drinking your juice. Enjoy the fresh, hydrating, potent and delicious concoction you have worked so hard to make, and be proud of yourself. This is pure healing medicine from Mother Nature for your body. That's your sweet reward for the hard work. I try to drink eight to twelve ounces right after juicing and right before cleanup.

As to how quickly or slowly to drink your juice, there are no hard and fast rules. I only insist that, if at all possible, you drink your juice on a relatively empty stomach. If I am really thirsty, I like to gulp it down. It's quick, and I don't want any of the potency to be lost. If you want to savor it, put it in a glass jar that has a lid you can close, just to keep it fresh as you enjoy it the next half hour or so.

Then comes the cleanup process. You must clean and wash your juicer *immediately* after use, except that little break you took to drink some of it. If you forget to clean your juicer right away, the colors from your produce will stain the juicer, and even though this would happen over time anyway, it will occur quicker if you neglect the cleanup process. My old Omega and Breville are both completely dishwasher safe, so after rinsing off as much of the produce as possible, I would throw them in the dishwasher. Not the case with the Greenstar, which needs to be hand washed. It has come equipped with all the necessary brushes so I just get to work and have it washed and set aside for drying in about ten minutes. It is work. It is effort. It's also not all that fun, but it's part of the commitment. You have made other commitments in your life and there are times when you just have to take care of business so you can continue to enjoy the privilege of the other times. So when it comes to washing your juicer after use, listen to Nike: just do it. Do it fast. Get it done with and move on!

If you have leftovers from your juice, read Chapter 8 for proper storage guidelines.

That concludes our walk-through process. You will need to add on firsthand experience to see how it compares, but I am willing to bet that after a dozen times of going through this process, you will have your own system and, even with small nuances of your own, you will agree that it's not that bad after all. This juicing business can become a lot of fun and hopefully a permanent habit in your life as you journey back to health and vitality.

JUICER IN THE SPOTLIGHT

Sarah Cornsnake, who loves juicing and dishing up new exotic recipes with the produce from her own backyard.

"I love the idea of doing something that is so healthy and good for my body. It all started when a friend of my husband's was diagnosed with Lyme disease and the only thing that gave her any relief was green juice. Before that, I had never heard of juicing. Now, after juicing, my weight has shifted in a positive direction. I am not eating differently on purpose but adding a juice into my day helps to keep me satisfied and eliminates some of the urges to snack. I also find myself craving the crisp uncomplicated flavors of juice."

The Recipes and the Benefits

Ready to dive into the recipes? I had a lot of fun putting this section together for us. Creating recipes is a fun adventure, but sharing them is the *best* part. The recipes come from a few sources. Most are directly from my own juicing experiments over the years. Some are favorites from the juicing community and other fellow juicing enthusiasts that I have met or interviewed. I have shared the contributor's names wherever applicable.

In Chapter 3, we talked about the three categories of juices: the fruit juices, the fruit and vegetable blends, the vegetable juices. This is the general approach to the recipe layout in this chapter. If you are a brand new juicer, start with the fruit juices and then move to the fruit and vegetable blends and then work your way up to the vegetable juices. This is the best way to ease into juicing but it's not a hard and fast rule. It's just a suggestion.

I have a friend who made a hard-core dark green all-vegetable juice, including a whole onion, as her *very first juice* and thought it was "not bad!" She was laughing as she described the strong taste but still enjoyed it and could not wait to experiment with new vegetables and combinations next time. And then there is my husband who needed to ease into juicing with fruit juices first, and then adding just one or two sweet vegetables; he is still slowly adjusting to the more green juices.

Plus there is a section on some fun pulp recipes, thanks to all who contributed from the community on their favorite uses of the post-juicing leftover pulp so it does not go to waste. If you want to get creative and have fun with using this fiber-rich pulp, check out some of those recipes.

So whether you sprint through this or take your time, have fun with it and mark your favorites in your juicing journal!

How to Best Use This Recipes Section

Those who think they have no time for healthy eating will sooner or later have to find time for illness.
~ Edward Stanley

I want to suggest that you first browse the whole recipes section once before making any of the recipes. This gives you a good idea what all your options are and familiarizes you with common fruit and vegetable combinations, benefits and measurements and who knows, you may just come across the perfect recipe that has all your favorite ingredients in one place and that may end up as your inaugural juice!

The recipes here make anywhere from three to five cups of juice. The actual amount varies depending on your size selection—what you may define as small, medium or large for whole fruits and vegetables—and your juicer—centrifugal juicer yields less than its masticating counterpart.

Serving size is up to you. I can happily drink several (four to eight) cups of green juice (vegetable juice category) a day! A good serving size is two full cups, and you can either chug it down or take your time to drink it slowly over 15–30 minutes. When you double your ingredients, you will more or less double the juice yield. You can also use half the ingredients and make half as much. This is a good idea if you are trying a brand new recipe and may not be sure if you will like the taste. Start out small and test it out!

As a general rule of thumb, you cannot drink *too much* vegetable juice. You should use your body reaction as your guiding light on whether you have had too little or too much. It is smart to limit your fruit juices or blends that are heavily fruit-based to one or at most two glasses a day.

Over time, most of us have developed a sense of what a "serving size" is for a particular food. One apple makes a good snack, and half of a cooked sweet potato is a good portion with a meal. But when juicing fruits and vegetables, the same servings cannot be applied because the resultant mass is much less due to the removal of all of the fiber from the fruits or vegetables; juicing half of a sweet potato wouldn't give your more than half a cup of juice in some cases and results vary from juicer to juicer.

So how do we determine how much juice is in our ingredients? The Internet is the place to go for this information. Computational search engines, such as Wolfram Alpha (www.wolframalpha.com), can give you a complete breakdown: the nutritional value, calories, mass, the serving volume for each of your ingredients and more. This is a method that my friend Israel Torres uses and has found this to be the most accurate search engine in this regard. Because fruits and vegetables come in many sizes, these numbers will be approximations, but still

Wolfram Alpha should give you a reasonable idea of what to expect for your recipes. Once you know the juice output from your individual ingredients, you can add them up together and get an idea of how much juice the whole recipe will make. Feel free to use this reference as you determine how much juice to make.

Also, unless otherwise noted, everything is unpeeled. If you need to peel something, I specifically mention it.

As a general rule, you can add ginger to just about *any* recipe. Use it sparingly and use small amounts when you start out. You can add garlic to most vegetable recipes; start with ½ or 1 clove and use this one sparingly as well.

Another tip is to use your citrus fruits—lemon and lime—in care-

ful quantities to start with. They go well together in the same recipe as well as are interchangeable if you have one or the other, but each adds a distinct taste. Lemons and limes add a lot of flavor and help to cut down the bitterness of dark leafy veggies. They also clean out your juicer so throw them in last.

You will notice that there are 11 recipes in the fruit juice section, 15 in the blends section and 20 in the vegetable juices section. The main reason for the division of numbers as such is that your fruit juices are where you start, then you move towards greener juices and when you get to the mainly vegetable juices, you will ideally "settle down" here and make these recipes most often. Hence more options in the last section!

Remember these two quick golden rules about recipes: First, you can always modify and second, things taste different when juiced together with other things than when eaten alone in whole raw form, so give new recipes and new combinations a chance. They can turn out surprisingly good! Have fun and happy juicing!

The Fruit Juices

The Quick and Dirty Flu Fighter
Ingredients:
2 small–medium oranges, peeled
1 small grapefruit, peeled
½ lemon
1 Yellow or Macintosh apple (or any other sweet apple)
A small chunk of ginger

Optional Additions:
A handful of parsley

Replacements:
1 cup peeled pineapple for apple

The Tart and Sweet Cooler

Ingredients:
1 cup cranberries
½ cup raspberries
2 cups pineapple, peeled

Optional Additions:
½ lemon

Replacements:
Use either cranberries or raspberries if you have only one.

The Lola Dreaming
Ingredients:
4 small Persian cucumbers
2 cups of baby spinach
A handful of mint
1 small yellow delicious apple
6–8 strawberries
1 lime
2 kiwis

Optional Additions:
A small chunk of ginger

Replacements:
Lemon for lime
Pear for apple

....

The Berry Melon Heaven
Ingredients:
10–12 strawberries
½–⅔ of a medium cantaloupe, peeled

Optional Additions:
A few chunks of pineapple

Replacements:
Honeydew for cantaloupe

The Sweet Pear Sensation
Ingredients:
2 small pears, any kind
1 medium sweet apple
2–4 stalks celery
½ lemon
A small chunk of ginger

Optional Additions:
3–4 strawberries or 4–5 raspberries

Replacements:
Pineapple for apple

··

The Wake Me Up Morning Cocktail
Ingredients:
2 cups fresh cranberries
2–3 medium carrots
A handful of cilantro
2 oranges, peeled
1 apple

Optional Additions:
2–4 strawberries or raspberries

Replacements:
Parsley or dill for cilantro
All oranges or all apples

The Pomegranate Pow Wow
Ingredients:
1 large pomegranate, peeled
½ to 1 lime
2 medium sweet apples, any kind

Optional Additions:
None

Replacements:
Lemon for lime

....

The Sunrise in Paradise
Ingredients:
2 mangoes, peeled
2 sweet delicious apples

Optional Additions:
2–4 strawberries
Ginger to taste

Replacements:
Pear for apple

The Pink Silk
Ingredients:
⅓ or ½ medium watermelon, peeled

Optional Additions:
A handful of fresh mint
½ lime

Replacements:
Basil or dill for mint leaves

. . . .

The Orange Ecstasy
Ingredients:
3–4 medium carrots
2 oranges, peeled
A small chunk of ginger

Optional Additions:
½ lemon

. . . .

The Ruby Rapture
Ingredients:
4 blood red oranges
8-10 strawberries

The Fruit and Vegetable Blends

The Ultimate Pineapple-Kale Blast
Ingredients
6–8 large leaves of kale with stem
½ large Italian cucumber
½ bunch parsley
2–2 ½ cups of pineapple chunks, peeled
¾ to 1 cup strawberries

Optional Additions:
A handful of fresh mint

Replacements:
Any other cucumber
Swiss chard for kale
Either a sweet apple for the strawberries or pineapple but not
   both

The Vitamin C Minty Rush
Ingredients:
3–4 cups baby spinach
A handful of parsley
2 small delicious apples
2 medium oranges, peeled
6–8 stems fresh mint
1 lemon
1 small chunk of ginger

Optional Additions:
1–2 small Persian cucumbers

Replacements:
Use all oranges or all apples

....

The Green Goddess
Ingredients:
7–8 large kale leaves
1 ½ –2 cups baby or regular spinach
12 strawberries
1 Granny smith medium–large apple
A handful of mint
¼ fennel, bulb and stalk
1 lime

Optional Additions
A handful of dill

Replacements:
Lemon for lime
Cilantro or parsley for mint

....

The Dapper Dan
Ingredients:
4 stalks Bok choy
2–4 broccoli crowns with short stalks
4–6 leaves of kale
1 cup green grapes
2–3 small Granny Smith apples
1 lemon

Optional Additions
1 small chunk of ginger

Replacements:
Lime for lemon
Spinach or collard greens for kale

The Emerald Deluxe

Ingredients:
2–3 cups of baby or regular spinach
3–4 stalks of celery
3–4 small Persian cucumbers
1 cup green or red grapes
1 large Granny Smith apple
A small chunk of ginger

Optional Additions:
A handful of fresh mint or dill

Replacements:
Any other cucumber
Collard greens or kale for spinach

The Green Explosion

Ingredients:
6–8 leaves of collard greens
1 medium Italian cucumber
A large handful of parsley
2 medium Granny Smith apples
1 medium orange, peeled
1 small Jalapeño pepper, seedless
½ lime

Optional Additions:
2 cloves of garlic, peeled
A chunk of ginger

Replacements:
Any other cucumber
Spinach or kale for collard greens

The Shanti Om Elixir

Ingredients:
A handful of cilantro
2–3 stalks celery
A small head of Romaine lettuce
4–6 leaves of Swiss chard
1 small red apple
1 medium yellow apple
½ lime
1 kiwi

Optional Additions:
Garlic and ginger to taste

Replacements:
Spinach for lettuce
Parsley for cilantro
Any other sweet apple to replace

The Frothy Monkey Juice

Ingredients:

⅓ of a large fennel

A bunch of mint

A small handful of watercress

4 large leaves of kale

A chunk of ginger

1–1½ cups of pineapple

8–10 strawberries

Optional Additions:

A chunk of turmeric

1–2 cloves of garlic, peeled

Replacements:

Spinach or collard greens for kale

A handful of dill or mint for fennel

The Smooth Sensation

Ingredients:
3–4 large leaves of Swiss chard
3–4 broccoli florets and stems
A small handful of parsley
½ large Italian cucumber
1 lemon
6–8 strawberries
2 small orchard apples

Optional Additions:
1–2 cloves of garlic, peeled
2–4 leaves basil

Replacements:
Any other cucumber
Any other sweet apple
Spinach or kale for Swiss chard

The Zen Dragonfly

Ingredients:
2–3 cups baby or regular spinach
A small head of Romaine lettuce
1 medium pear
1 medium Granny Smith apple
8–10 strawberries

Optional Additions:
Ginger and garlic to taste

Replacements:
Raspberries for strawberries
Pears for apples and vice versa

....

The Emerald Fantasy
Ingredients:
1 grapefruit, peeled
1 orange, peeled
1 Honey Crisp (or any other) apple
2 stalks and ¼ bulb of fennel
½ bunch basil
½ bunch cilantro
1 large Italian cucumber
1 small chunk of raw turmeric

Optional Additions:
Ginger and garlic to taste

Replacements:
Any other cucumber
All grapefruit or all orange

The Unbelievably Creamy Lush Dream

Ingredients:
1 large sweet potato, peeled
2 medium red apples
3–4 medium size carrots

Optional Additions:
1 Jalapeño pepper, seedless

Replacements:
Any other sweet apple
Cayenne pepper for Jalapeño

The Perfect Simple Essence

Ingredients:
2 Roma or other type tomatoes
3–4 carrots
1 small yellow or red sweet bell pepper, seedless
2 Persian cucumbers
1 small chunk ginger

Optional Additions:
1 small handful parsley
1 clove garlic, peeled

Replacements:
Any other cucumber

The Sexy Sassy Surprise

Ingredients:
3–4 carrots
1 medium head of Romaine lettuce
8–10 strawberries
1 medium or large pear
1 handful of fresh basil
½–1 lime

Optional Additions:
1–2 cloves garlic, peeled

Replacements:
Any other lettuce except iceberg
Lemon for lime
Mint or fennel for basil

The Yellow Sunset

Ingredients:
2–2 ½ cups Baby or regular spinach
¼ fennel bulb and stalk
2 small oranges, peeled
1–1 ½ cups mango, peeled

Optional Additions:
A handful of fresh mint or basil

Replacements:
Apple for mango

The Vegetable Juices

The Juice on the Rush
Ingredients
4 carrots
4–6 stalks of celery
1 large cucumber
1 apple

Optional Additions:
A small chunk of ginger

Replacements:
None

The Rich Red Cleanse
Ingredients
2–3 medium carrots
1 medium beet
4–5 stalks of celery
1 large Macintosh or Honey Crisp apple
A handful of parsley
1 lemon

Optional Additions:
1 clove garlic, peeled

Replacements:
Cilantro for parsley
Tomatoes for apples

....

The Hydrating Refresher
Ingredients:
1 ½ to 2 cups of baby spinach
3–4 small Persian cucumbers
1 cup of arugula
2 medium Roma tomatoes
1 lemon
1 small chunk of ginger

Optional Additions:
A handful of basil

Replacements:
Lime for lemon
Parsley for cilantro

....

The Popeye Infusion
Ingredients:
3–4 cups of baby spinach
2–4 stalks celery
1 Macintosh apple
¼ fennel bulb and stalk
½ large Italian cucumber
1 lemon

Optional Additions:
1–2 cloves garlic, peeled
1 chunk of ginger

Replacements:
Pear for apple

The Sweet Filling Delight
Ingredients:
3 cups of baby spinach
A handful of basil
2 small sweet apples
2–3 medium carrots
½ bunch parsley
½ sweet potato, peeled

Optional Additions:
A handful (4–6) carrot top greens to make it less sweet

Replacements:
Cilantro for parsley
Dill or mint for basil

The Hawaiian Rainbow
Ingredients:
4–5 small carrots
2 small or 1 large beet
1 cup baby spinach
1 cup arugula
A handful of parsley
2 small oranges, peeled

Optional Additions:
A handful (4–6) carrot top greens to make it less sweet
1–2 cloves of garlic

Replacements:
Lettuce for arugula
Apple for orange

The Great Grassy Punch
Ingredients:
14 oz. container of wheatgrass (organically grown)
1 Granny Smith apple
A small chunk of ginger
Yields exactly 2 shot glasses

The Reboot Essentials

Ingredients:

½ small white or green cabbage head

3–4 medium carrots

2 cups of spinach

1 small handful of watercress

1–2 cloves garlic

1 small ginger chunk

1 small turmeric chunk

1 lemon

Optional Additions:

1 medium sweet apple

½ cayenne pepper

Replacements:

Swiss chard for spinach

Parsley for watercress

The Perfect Purifier
Ingredients:
1 medium beet
¼ of cabbage head
2 Persian cucumbers
1 medium parsnip
A handful of parsley
1 large yellow or red sweet apple
1 lime

Optional Additions:
A handful (2–3) beet top greens to make it less sweet
Ginger and garlic to taste

Replacements:
Lemon for lime
Carrots for parsnip

The Crystal Clean Lagoon
Ingredients:
A large cucumber
A small handful of parsley
3–4 stalks of celery
3–4 medium carrots
1 small sweet pear
2 stalks and ¼ bulb of fennel
1 whole Belgian endive

Optional Additions:
A small handful of watercress
A small chunk of turmeric
1–2 cloves of garlic, peeled

Replacements:
More carrots for Belgian endive
Apple for pear
Any other cucumbers

The Multi Nutri Juice

Ingredients:
6 leaves of Swiss chard
⅔ to 1 beet
3–4 medium carrots
4 Roma tomatoes
A handful of parsley
1–2 small cucumbers
1 lemon
A chunk of ginger

Optional Additions:
1–2 cloves of garlic, peeled
A handful (2–3) beet top greens to make it less sweet

Replacements:
Celery for cucumbers
Kale for Swiss chard

The Complete Winter Healer

Ingredients:

4–5 leaves of Swiss chard
3–4 leaves of lettuce
2–3 medium carrots
1 medium beet
2–3 small cucumbers
2 Roma tomatoes
1 bunch watercress
½ lime or lemon
2 cloves garlic, peeled
A chunk of ginger

Optional Additions:

A handful (2–3) beet top greens to make it less sweet
A handful (2–3) carrot top greens to make it less sweet

Replacements:

Parsley for watercress
Spinach for Swiss chard

The Highly Potent Pallooza

Ingredients:

4 stalks celery

1 cup spinach

3–4 broccoli florets and stems

½ bunch parsley

2 small Granny Smith green apples

2 cloves garlic

1 small chunk ginger

1 jalapeño pepper, seedless

Optional Additions:

1 small chunk turmeric

Replacements:

Cilantro for parsley

Carrot for apples

The Super Detox Galore

Ingredients:
6-8 leaves kale
4-6 stalks celery
1 whole Belgian endive
½ white onion
2 small red delicious apples
½ lemon or lime
1 chunk ginger
2 cloves of garlic
1 cayenne pepper

Optional Additions:
1 small handful watercress

Replacements:
Collard greens for kale
Cabbage for Belgian endive

Red and Green Heavenly Concoction

Ingredients:
3–4 medium carrots
6–8 leaves kale
⅓ fennel stalk and bulb
½ dill or mint bunch
3–4 Roma tomatoes
3–4 florets of broccoli
½ large Italian cucumber
1 lemon

Optional Additions:
½ bunch watercress
1–2 cloves garlic, peeled

Replacements:
Spinach for kale
Dill for cilantro

The Hot Mamma Green Juice
Ingredients:
2 Roma tomatoes
2–3 medium carrots
2 small parsnips
1 Italian cucumber
1 cup baby spinach
1 small handful cilantro
1 small handful parsley
¼ fennel
1 small cayenne pepper (or spice powder to taste)

Optional Additions:
Garlic and ginger to taste

Replacements:
More parsley for cilantro or vice versa
Jalapeño pepper for cayenne pepper
More carrots for the parsnips

The Peaceful Warrior

Ingredients:
4–6 leaves kale
2–4 medium carrots
1 cup of baby spinach
1 cup of arugula
2–4 broccoli florets and stem
3–4 leaves dandelion
2 medium oranges, peeled

Optional Additions:
Garlic and ginger to taste

Replacements:
Watercress for dandelion
Romaine lettuce for arugula

Excitement in Your Mouth Juice

Ingredients:
2 sweet potatoes, peeled
3–4 carrots
1 small cayenne pepper (or cayenne pepper powder to taste)

Optional Additions:
1–2 carrots

Replacements:
Apples for carrots

The Feast of a Champion
Ingredients:
1 sweet potato, peeled
2–3 Roma tomatoes
1 small beet
2 medium carrots
2–3 broccoli florets and stem
A handful of parsley
½ white or purple onion
1 small chunk ginger
2 cloves garlic

Optional Additions:
1 small chunk of turmeric

Replacements:
Celery for broccoli
Apple for tomato

The Whole Enchilada
Ingredients:
3–4 leaves kale
3–4 leaves Romaine lettuce
1 cup spinach
1 cup arugula
A handful of parsley
A handful of basil
A handful of dandelion
1 cup pineapple
8-10 strawberries
1 small chunk ginger

Optional Additions:
1 small chunk of turmeric
1 Jalapeño pepper

Replacements:
Green collards for kale or spinach

The Aftermath: You've Juiced. Now What?

First of all, congratulations! You have finished juicing all those beautiful and colorful fruits and vegetables, and enjoyed your glass of a green—or orange or red or other color—juice. Wonderful! Be super proud of yourself. This is an accomplishment every single time so take a minute to do your celebration dance and savor the moment—and the juice!

Now what happens next? And when does the cleanup fairy show up to make the aftermath of juicing a most memorable experience?

Well, I haven't met my cleanup fairy yet but the happiness and joy that comes over me after drinking my green goodness pushes me to the finish line of taking care of all the remaining business, from cleanup to storage and reassembly of the juicer. I bet you will feel some of this buzz too.

One of the big questions in the post-juicing stage is whether you can store your juice or not? Some experts advocate that you must you drink it all right away, but is that approach practical with our busy lives and will it help us establish a regular routine of juicing? This is a big decision to make as you get more into juicing because it takes some planning, time and effort to juice, as you

know well by now, and you may want to drink juice every day but not go through the hassle of making it every single time. We talk about all that in this chapter.

The other question is what on earth to do with all that fresh pulp that your fruits and vegetables leave behind? Can you make any use of it? Does it depend on the juicer or the type of pulp? And how can you get creative so you have no waste from the whole juicing process?

Dive into this chapter to get answers to those questions and more. I will see you there!

To Store or Not to Store, That Is the Question!

If hunger is not the problem, then eating is not the solution.
~ Unknown

Most juicing experts say that you *should* consume your juice immediately or within the first hour of making it—and this is great advice because the juice is at its freshest and most potent then. But does this mean you have to go through all that trouble every time you want a glass of juice? What if you make more than you can drink at one sitting? Is there anything you can do to make it last a bit longer?

The question is to store or not to store your juice! Fresh juice is fresh only for so long and you want to drink it up to get the benefits of the live enzymes and the high potency of your juice right away. No argument there! But I want to add that under certain conditions, you can and in fact should store your juice.

Condition Number One is that you need to use a masticating juicer to be able to store your juice, because this juicer gives you the highest quality juice that will not oxidize quickly. You can store in these conditions for up 36 hours in the refrigerator. If you store the juice more than 36 hours, it does not go "bad" or make you sick or anything like that. It just won't have as many nutrients and as much potency as it does immediately after it comes out of the juicer. It will be more flat and have less of that "wow" factor, but it will still be fine. Under 36 hours, it's perfectly fine as long as you also meet Condition Number Two!

Condition Number Two is that you must use a glass jar container, not plastic, and one that has an airtight lid to keep it fresh. Invest in one or two glass jar containers and use them only for juicing and no other purposes. Plastic containers develop a terrible smell and this smell rubs off on your juice over time. Plus your plastic containers turn a yellow brown color if you use them to store your juice. Nothing beats an airtight-lid glass container. Use these glass containers exclusively for your juice and nothing else.

One of the reasons that I want to encourage you to store your juice at the very least over-night is because, as you are first establishing this habit of juicing, it can be challenging. Sure, ideally you should juice *every single day* including weekends—I know even hard-core juicers who juice more than once a day—but let's get practical here. We have busy lives and this is yet one more thing that takes time and energy. If you make it impossible to achieve, you will put it aside after two or three tries and never look back. I want to give you all the tools to make this a practical habit to integrate into your busy life and storing your juice for up to 36 hours can hopefully help you ease into this habit.

One vegetable to be careful about storing is cabbage juice. If you use cabbage in any of your recipes, try to drink it all right away. When you store cabbage juice—even if mixed with other ingredients—it can smell *very* unpleasant in your fridge and that smell permeates to your other foods. Avoid storing cabbage and all vegetables in the family of cabbage. You can check out which falls in that category by looking them up on Wikipedia.

It takes some courage and determination to integrate this juicing habit into your life but you totally can do it. I gave up on it several times before making it a non-negotiable part of my lifestyle. What helped me was making it more practical, and if you can stretch your juice further and take a break from going through the process every single day, you are far more likely to continue the habit. Plus drinking that juice the next day reminds you how much you love this stuff, how good it is for your body, and you will be

anxious to get back in the kitchen after a day or two of rest to make your next batch of green goodness.

If you have only a centrifugal machine, then some of the benefits are that it is faster and that you do not need to chop your fruits and veggies so small because the chute is larger than the masticating types. It's perfectly fine to start out with a centrifugal machine and then move up to the more reliable kind such as the masticating types. You should try to drink all the juice you make using this machine and not store it, but since you are also more likely to use it frequently because it's easier and quicker, that may balance out the storage limitation!

What to Do with All That Pulp

Cheerfulness, sir, is the principle ingredient
in the composition of health.
~ Arthur Murphy

Now we come to some of the additional benefits of the juicing revolution—all the things you can do with the pulp of the fruits and vegetables from your juicing. I feel guilty when I don't use all my leftover pulp, knowing just how much I could be doing with it! I had so much fun putting together all the best uses of pulp here for us in this section.

The pulp is what your juicer extracts from your fruits and vegetables. It has fresh amounts of fiber that is extremely good for your body. Fiber that passes through your digestive system helps other foods pass through more easily and it is essential in its own cleansing properties for your body.

Here's one of the advantages of having a centrifugal juicer over a masticating one: Your pulp will be less dry and retain more juice and flavor and you will be able to make much better use of it.

You can do so much with your pulp and get so creative. Below I have listed the top 12 uses depending on what you enjoy doing—baking, cooking, making soups or salads, feeding your pet and so much more. So no matter what, there should be a use for your pulp that matches your lifestyle preferences.

Just follow these three quick rules of thumb:
1. Best option: Use the pulp right away after juicing if possible. The sooner you use the pulp, the fresher!
2. Second best option: Store it right away in a zip-top bag or an airtight container in the fridge for up to two days.
3. Third best option: Freeze the pulp in a zip-top bag for a week or ten days.

Top 12 uses for your leftover pulp:

1. **Put it in your compost:** If you have no other use for it and are not into baking, cooking, or interested in using the pulp, then please use it in your compost. It is much better than putting it in the garbage. Some people bury the pulp into the soil around their plants as fertilizers. Plants have the amazing ability to reconstruct the minerals from the pulp into organic materials that are suitable for their growth.

2. **Make a delicious vegetable broth:** An easy way to use leftover vegetable pulp is to make homemade broth. Making homemade vegetable broth is one of my hubby's favorite ways to use juice pulp. Use only your vegetable pulp here, not any fruit pulp. You can include ginger, garlic, and herb pulp though. Your stock will have great flavor, especially if your pulp is not too dry.

3. **Add it to soups:** Along with vegetable broth, you can add the vegetable pulp directly to your soups to give it more body. Store vegetable pulp in the freezer (along with any other veggie scraps or peels) and throw them right in when ready to use.

4. **Add it to your smoothies:** Your fruit pulp especially will add a good source of fiber to your smoothie, and if you use your pulp from a centrifugal juicer, it will add tons of moisture to the smoothie. The berry and apple pulp is best for this use, especially if you have some frozen banana as your smoothie base. Yum!

5. **Mix it in your kid's foods:** This is a great and sneaky way to add some fiber goodness to your kids' foods without changing the flavor of their food too much for them to notice. Carrot pulp can work well in their macaroni and cheese or their mashed potatoes, too.

6. **Bake a large variety of baked goods and breads with it:** One of the most popular ways to use pulp from apples, carrots, and zucchini is for baked goods. Use pulp in standard recipes for things like apple muffins, zucchini bread, and carrot cake, or add to other baked goods to increase moisture—in many cases, you can even decrease the amount of oil a recipe calls for when using fruit pulp. The vegetable pulp will also cut down the sweetness in the baked goods and make them healthier!

7. **Toss it over your salads:** My two favorite pulps for this are beet and carrot pulp—they have beautiful color and texture and I add them liberally onto salads. They don't have much flavor by themselves—mine is usually very dry pulp—but the dressing and the other salad parts take care of that and it makes for a fiber-rich salad. I don't use the dark leafy vegetable pulp because of the stringy-like way it comes out that keeps it from mixing well into salads.

8. **Use it in your stuffing, pasta, lasagna, burgers or meat loaf:** When making meals like meatloaf, burgers (veggie or meat) and meatballs, vegetable pulp from celery, carrots, beets or spinach comes in really handy. Adding the leftover pulp gives extra fiber

and moisture to the dish. You can add your carrot, spinach, beet, or other types of pulp to spaghetti sauce or layer it into lasagna. Remember, beet has a strong dark red color and it may take over the color of the rest of your food more so than other pulps.

9. Make raw crackers and baked goods with your dehydrator: If you have a dehydrator, you can find tons of recipes on how to make raw crackers and other raw baked goods with pulp. You can use any kind of vegetable pulp for this.

10. Use it as topping for pancakes, omelets, waffles or other desserts: Throw some of that pulp into your pancakes, especially from the berries and the apples. You can also add these fruit pulps to your waffle mix or other desserts. They add moisture, flavor and a nice texture. You can also mix pulp into your omelets; carrot and spinach and tomato pulp would do well here.

11. Use it in dips and sauces: If you enjoy making dips and sauces, especially in your blender, you can use your vegetable pulp such as spinach, kale, tomato, carrots and the like in a great vegetable dip. If you find recipes online that call for the vegetables, just replace one or two of them with the pulp of that recipe and you are good to go.

12. Use them in your dog or pet food or make dog biscuits with it: Talk to your vet about your individual pet's diet before feeding them the pulp. To make a Doggy Dinner, just add your daily pulp to pooch's food. Mix it in with either dry or wet food.

They will enjoy the benefits of increased fiber and the nutrient density and it gives them a change in flavor too.

So these are some ideas on what to do with your pulp, but if you are in a hurry or can't get excited about using your pulp, don't feel bad. I have had to throw mine away on occasion. Bottom line: Don't let your plans about the pulp affect your juicing habit. Juice as often and on every occasion that you get and if you can do something with the pulp, then bonus! If not, store it or don't worry. Your body will love you for the juice and there's always more pulp in the future, so worry not and juice on!

The Pulp Recipes

Quick Pulp Ideas:
Toss carrot and beet pulp on your green salads.
Add carrot pulp to any cole slaw recipe.
Parsley and cilantro pulp make an excellent "minced herb" to add to a tossed salad, especially when using olive oil and a balsamic reduction as a salad dressing.

Deva's Fruit Pulp Muffins

Dry Ingredients:
1 ½ cups flour
½ cup oatmeal
¼ cup sugar
1 tsp. baking soda
1 tsp. baking powder
½ tsp. salt

Instructions:
Mix all dry ingredients together in a large bowl.

Wet Ingredients:
Fruit pulp
1 or 2 mashed ripe bananas
1 tsp. vanilla
½ cup liquid (water, skim milk, or almond milk)

Instructions:
Mix wet ingredients together. You should have about 1 ½ cups of fruit (pulp plus the banana).
Add wet ingredients to dry and mix until flour is well blended but not smooth. Muffin batter should always be a bit lumpy.
Bake at 350° Fahrenheit for 15–20 minutes.

Sandi's Creamy Mushroom Soup

Ingredients:
Green juice pulp
1 lb. mushrooms, sliced
1 onion chopped
2 garlic cloves, chopped
Salt and pepper to taste
1 tsp. herbes de provence
½ cup of milk

Instructions:
Sauté chopped onion and garlic in a soup pot on medium heat. Add mushrooms and green pulp and cook five minutes longer with lid on. Once mushrooms have begun to soften, add about a liter of water and bring to a boil. If you prefer a creamy soup, remove from heat and blend (either in glass blender or with hand mixer.) Return to heat and add seasonings and milk. Cover and cook on low heat for 20 to 30 minutes. Optional: Serve with grated sharp cheddar.

Amorim's Thai Curry Spinach Soup

Ingredients:
1 onion diced
2–3 cloves of garlic, minced finely
2–3 regular potatoes, chopped
1 cup fresh spinach
1 tsp. Red Thai curry paste (more if you like heat!)
Green veggie pulp (kale, spinach, celery, tomato, ginger, carrot, or any similar combination)

Instructions:
Sauté onion and garlic in a tablespoon of olive oil until golden. Add potatoes and pulp. After a quick stir, add a few cups of water (approx. 4–6 depending on the size of your soup pot) and add the fresh spinach. Bring to a boil. Lower heat and simmer for 10–15 minutes. Remove the pot from the heat and puree with a hand mixer, but you could also do so in a blender if it's a glass container. Once puréed, pour back into soup pot and season. Cover and simmer awhile longer. And voila! Yummy soup made from your veggie pulp!

```
NOTE

• Both the Regina's Strawberry Jam and Crema's Yummy
  Apple Butter recipes below use fairly dry pulp from
  juiced fruits indicated. The end result was delicious.
  Because some juicers yield drier pulp, the water con-
  tent for each recipe may vary.
• These recipes are not intended to be canned or pre-
  served. Canning and preserving requires specific steps
  that are not in these recipes. Keep refrigerated.
```

Regina's Strawberry Jam

Ingredients:
Pulp from a large carton of fresh strawberries that have been
    juiced.
¼ cup brown sugar
1–3 cups water (depending on dryness and wetness of your pulp)
2 tbsp. fresh lemon juice

Instructions:
Combine all ingredients in a pot and bring to a boil. Then cover
and let simmer on low for about an hour or until the jam thickens
up. Let cool, then enjoy! Can be refrigerated.

Crema's Yummy Apple Butter

Ingredients:
The pulp from 3–4 apples that have been peeled and juiced
2–3 cups cold filtered water
¼ cup raw or organic honey, local if possible
½ cup brown sugar
1 tbsp. cinnamon
½ to 1 whole stick of butter
1 tbsp. Meyer's Lemon Juice

Instructions:
Lemon juice keeps the apples from turning brown. You can do fresh squeezed lemon juice or use Meyer's brand. Add all ingredients into a pot and let simmer on low heat for about one hour or until desired consistency. You may need to add more or less water depending on how dry your apple pulp is. You may also add more or less of any of the above ingredients to suit your personal taste and dietary needs. Also, the types of apple you use will affect the taste of the apple butter. For example, Granny Smith apples will yield a more sour and tangy apple butter than you would get when using a sweet Golden Delicious or a Honey Crisp apple.

JUICER IN THE SPOTLIGHT

Sandi Amorim, who came to juicing with reservations and now has fallen in love with it and enjoys her second juicer, Juicy Lucy, daily.

"I spent a couple of months thinking about juicing before I decided to take it on. I had concerns like, "Would I be able to do it?" and "How long could I keep it going?" But my curiosity was stronger than my concerns and I knew I had to do it! What got me thinking about it in the first place was a strong desire to make health my focus this year. I began with a pretty intense detox and realized in the first week that juicing would be the perfect complement. And it has been, easing much of the challenge of completely trans-forming how I shop, cook and eat! After three weeks of juicing, my chiropractor asked what was going on because the energy she was feeling in my back was. . . .I think she called it zingy! My backache had decreased greatly, and the chronic throbbing in my hip was almost gone. Not kid-ding."

How to Improvise: Making Your Own Recipes

Modify recipes shamelessly. That is correct, my dear juicing enthusiast! Recipes are simply guidelines, they are someone else's experiment all measured up and written out. They are open to modification, and I highly encourage you to take charge during your juicing journey and try as many new recipes and new ingredients as possible and *always* be modifying recipes and guidelines to your taste and desire.

You have my full permission and total blessing for modifying any of the recipes in this book. Go for it! You are the juice boss and your taste buds are king and I am happy for you no matter how you get your juice in.

So in this chapter, we talk about why and how your taste buds can guide you to the right taste and flavor at the right time for you, plus we will cover some quick and easy ways you can improvise recipes to make them truly your own special edition.

It may take you a little while to get the hang of this. Being able to tell all the different flavors in a juice is your first task so get used to just finding all the flavors first. Then develop your taste buds over time so you can tell which flavor is too strong and which one is barely there, and then play with the measurements.

You never know when you will come up with a master recipe that everyone else will want to get their hands on because you modified it to perfection, guided by your own taste buds and curiosity. Some of the newcomers to my juicing clinic were shocked when I would tell them that soon, they were going to give *me* ideas and recipes on juicing. Sure enough, two weeks or less into the clinic, they would be experimenting in the kitchen and coming up with brand new combinations that I had never thought of or a new fruit or vegetable that I had not yet juiced myself. I love that we are constantly learning about juicing.

Oh the fun that awaits you! Roll up your sleeves and get confident, because you are about to kick it up a notch and get creative in the kitchen. We'll just cover some basic tips and guidelines in this chapter to show you how best to improvise, baby! Let's get ready to learn how you can make your own recipes, create your own concoctions and be your own juicing champion.

Your Taste Buds Are King: Juice What You Know First

Nature performs the cure, the physician takes the fee.
~ Benjamin Franklin

I vividly remember a scene in the movie *The Thomas Crown Affair* when the Rene Russo character, a top-notch police investigator, ordered this dark green, slushy, thick liquid concoction for breakfast, and I felt nauseated to my stomach just watching her slurp it. Yuck! It was a long while before I could get the image out of my head, and until I had made my own new association between that color and the word *delicious*, I couldn't even consider drinking that stuff.

You may not realize how powerful your imagination can be for the role that food plays in your mind, and the associations that you form long before it even enters your mouth. I have often regretted the stories I made up about other cultures' foods only to find out that reality is quite different. For instance, I really missed out on Indian food and sushi and other delicacies for much too long! What may not *look* very appetizing based on your preconceived notions can in fact be the most delicious food to your taste buds.

How can you not miss out then on the best and greatest tastes in the world? How can you let your taste buds be king and tell you the truth if you are afraid of actual experience?

First, you must make a conscious choice to be open to experimenting. Tasting a little of something can be a harmless, effective and easy way to find out whether you like it or not. You then establish it as a fact, not a guess. You can know for certain how *you* feel about a particular food or drink, not how your mom or your sister or your best friend feels but how *you* feel. This is empowering.

When it comes to juices, especially the greener and darker colors that you may not be familiar with, make sure your imagination is *not making things up* about them before you have had the invaluable insight from firsthand experience. The good news is that you will quickly get over the color when you get to the delicious taste. You just have that initial mental barrier to work through.

Let's break this down by a little exercise.

We start with acknowledging and then releasing the first thoughts that come to your mind: A dark green, brown, rich red drink may not look *appetizing* or taste *good*. Acknowledged. Check.

Now how do we release these thoughts? Ask yourself why do you have them in the first place? You may have them simply because you have not ever had a drink of that color. Your mind has not yet formed a positive association between the drink and your taste buds and therefore, it is free to create a new association based on what it sees on the surface: color, texture, density. It may search your memory for something similar and when nothing comes up, it makes the worst assumption from the fear of exposing you to something that *may* not taste good.

Release these thoughts by reminding yourself that you have no proof and you would like a little proof in order to establish this feeling for certain.

Then you are ready to find proof and the way you do that is through firsthand experience with those fabulous taste buds in your mouth. So now you have no choice but to smell and taste your drink to create this *new and real association.*

So we first acknowledged, second released and third created a new association in your mind about the juice.

Now that we have the exercise out of the way, let us talk about actual experience. What if you have had a bad experience with vegetable juices in the past? What if you have tried a juice before and found the taste to be bitter, strong, pungent and even nauseating? I hear you and I have too, several times, but there is a way to recreate a fresh new memory.

For instance, a bad juicing experience may have been with bottled juices. Remind yourself that bottled juice have little to nothing in common with fresh juices as far as taste, benefits and flavors go. Assure yourself that the fresh juices are entirely different. The experience will be different. The taste will be different and the way you will feel about it will also be different.

The next scenario is that you actually have had a fresh glass of green juice—maybe you even made it yourself—and it tasted icky and that was that, you have sworn to never have anything to do with a green juice again. Or maybe you mixed a few fruits to make a fruit juice that didn't taste good and you moved on to smoothies or raw foods. Maybe the juice gave you a bad bellyache; maybe your body started to make strange noises, you needed a few unexpected trips to the bathroom and the overall reaction was plain negative.

In this case, your taste buds absolutely told you the truth *but* something else may have gone awry that you can fix. Maybe you can turn the situation around.

Ask yourself: Is it possible that you made a recipe that did not settle well with you? Or you had the drink on a full-stomach as opposed to an empty one so the juice didn't settle well with the lunch you had an hour ago? Or could there have been too much of one ingredient or too little of another?

The answer is *yes*. All those could be true and none of them means that your next green juice will be the same experience. In fact, it's impossible! Remember the rule to give everything at least two good chances? Well, if your first experience was a bad one, give it one more chance and this time choose a recipe based on familiarity: Juice what you know first.

Juice what you know first means that you go with vegetables and fruits that you know you enjoy eating as whole, and start with a simpler recipe such as a 50-50 blend using these familiar ingredients. The combined taste will be different than the taste of eating a fruit or vegetable by itself, yes, but it will be familiar and that's what you are counting on! Also, start with a small quantity. One cup or a half a cup of juice will be more than enough for your taste buds and your stomach when you are first starting out. And this is where you want to really listen to your taste buds.

How do you listen to your taste buds anyway? What exactly does it mean? Let's break it down further with the **3 As**:

1. **Aroma**: I want you to first smell your drink. Green juices have a strong aroma and smelling my juice is one of my favorite things to do. Just take in the smell, see if you can guess the ingredients, and familiarize yourself with this new smell.

2. **Awareness:** Pay attention with *total* awareness when you taste your juice. How does it taste? Is it sweet, sour, bitter, sharp, smooth, pungent or rich? Is it a new taste you can learn to love? Does it go down easily? Take small sips and swish it in your mouth and try to describe it. Take it in like it's an expensive glass of wine at a wine tasting party!

3. **Attitude**: We have an attitude towards *everything* in life and fruits and vegetables are no exception. Whatever your encounters in the past, leave them behind if only temporarily and take an impartial fresh attitude towards this new experience and create new memories. Stop the inner chatter in your mind and just take in the unadulterated juice. How is it?

Another thing to keep in mind is that your taste buds *change*. Even though they told you the truth about the "icky" juice you had eons ago because it was perhaps too "strong" or "pungent" at the time, they can change yet! You can develop your taste buds to the point where you will find that same drink not only tolerable but also delicious. I never advocate that you drink a disgusting tasting juice just to get the benefits. I want to remind you that your taste buds can adapt over time and you can develop more of a taste for stronger greener juicer. You might even have less of a taste for the fruitier, sweeter juices over time.

The higher your tolerance for the greener juices with higher vegetable content and lesser fruit content, the faster and further the benefits of true juicing will go for you. This is the ideal state to aspire to reach in the juicing journey, and it's all pure fun as long as you have willingness to explore and experiment and stay true to your own guiding taste buds.

So rest assured, not all juices are created equal. There will be some that you won't initially care for and that's fine. There are some that will grow on you after a while if you keep trying them and there are others that will be your absolute favorites. So remember to go with what you know first, to do it on a relatively empty stomach and to start with small quantities. When you follow these guidelines, you will ease into your juicing experience.

Then let your taste buds guide you. They are king. Always trust your own taste buds to tell you how you feel about a juice and keep tasting until you find your favorites.

The Art and Science of Creating Your Own Recipes

If I'd known I was going to live so long, I'd have taken
better care of myself.
*~ **Leon Eldred***

If you want to stick with juicing for the long haul, you need to make it as much *fun* as possible, and one way to do that is to feel OK going against the traditional way of doing things once in a while. Sometimes, that means mixing it up in the kitchen with total disregard to recipes and rules and creating your very own custom-made recipes. Other times, it may mean a single yet substantial modification to a recipe that was intolerable to you until you customized it to your own needs with this one change. There is both an art and a science to creating your own recipes. The science part I want to cover here and the art, well, that's entirely up to you!

A recipe is just a suggestion based on someone else's experiment. I would love to glorify my recipes here. After all, they are my heart-felt suggestions based on years of experimenting and exploring the juicing world. These are the combination formulae that have worked well for me and my juicing community but they are simply suggestions, and in the end you decide if you like them.

As a beginner, I want to encourage you to start with simpler juices; that means juices that are easier for your body for acclimation and absorption. These are juices whose ingredients you have already tasted as a whole raw form, not exotic new fruits and vegetables that you've not yet tried. The two new elements here are first, the juice form versus the whole raw form and second, the combination of several juices that creates a brand new taste.

General rule of thumb: If the recipe tastes too strong or bitter, add more of your base fruit or the sweeter vegetables such as tomato, carrot or beets, or less of the dark leafy vegetables. If it's not enough of one vegetable and too much of another, like if you only taste the celery and none of the kale, then modify accordingly, reduce the fruit or the sweeter vegetables until you are happy with the taste.

If your intention for juicing is to detox and cleanse, get to know what I call your Four Detox and Healing Galore ingredients: garlic, ginger, turmeric and pepper (Jalapeño is my favorite), all in raw forms. These four amazing ingredients, rich in anti-inflammatory anti-oxidant content, alone or combined, can make a potent hot powerful juice! The healing and medicinal properties of this foursome are endless and it would behoove you to make friends with them. Unlike your random vegetable or fruit that you may dislike, do what you can to make friends with these four. Start adding each in tiny quantities and separately at first to your juices and go from there.

Garlic is delicious and adds a strong flavor to a bland juice. Ginger, even in small quantities, creates heat in your body and has a sharp pungent taste, but it doesn't stick around like hot pepper on your tongue. It's more like its sushi companion wasabi, the Japanese horseradish sauce. It may make you cry and sniff but it's gone as soon as it's arrived and it has cleaned up all the mess along the way. Pepper is hot and adds excitement to your juice. Turmeric, also known as the Sacred Spice in the East, is sweet and flavorful and adds a touch of rich taste to your juices.

When you create your own recipes from scratch, think in terms of the juice categories in this book: Fruit Juices, the Fruit and Vegetable Blends and Vegetable Juices. What are you in the mood for? If you want a sweeter juice or juice as dessert, then stick to

fruits, but drink in moderation to limit the sugar intake. If you want greener and more filling drinks, add vegetables.
Start with a base for your juice. Good bases are:

* Tomatoes
* Apples
* Pears
* Oranges
* Carrots
* Beets
* Combination of the above

Then add your secondary ingredients depending on the type of juice you are making (Fruit, Fruit and Vegetable Blends or Vegetable).

Then add your herbs, if you want. Think of them as your "spices"; add until you get the right taste for you. Your most common herbs are:

* Cilantro
* Parsley
* Fennel
* Mint
* Basil
* Dill

> **This is your rescue tip:** Taste a sip and if it's not to your liking, then simply add one more of your base depending on the flavor direction you need to go.

And again if you want, add any of the Four Detox and Healing Galore ingredients in small quantities:
- Garlic
- Ginger
- Turmeric
- Hot pepper

In summary, here are the basic guidelines we just covered on creating your own recipe:
- Add two parts of your base.
- Add one part your secondary ingredient of vegetable/fruit.
- Add half a part your herbs.
- Add a pinch or a dash of your Four Detox and Healing Galore ingredients.
- Add one part additional base if the taste is not quite right.

An example:

Base: 2 carrots
Secondary ingredient: 1 cup spinach
Herb: small handful parsley
Detox ingredient: a quarter size of ginger
Additional base: 1 small apple

Now if a fruit or vegetable or herb does not make your taste buds happy, then stop juicing it. You have to learn how to single them out through a process of elimination and you will get good at it fast with trial and error. Skip that ingredient even if a recipe calls for it. If your body doesn't like it after a couple of tries, then stop juicing it altogether or change the ingredients of the juice to make it less bitter, or less sharp and pungent, or more or less sweet (playing natural sweeteners like carrot and apple and orange), especially for recipes that call for dark leafy vegetables and herbs.

You can modify the recipes in three ways:

1. You can **adjust** the quantity of each ingredient and still keep all ingredients in; this way, you get exposure to all the components making up the recipe but adjust the ratios initially to suit your taste buds.
2. You can **take out** one or more ingredients to simplify the taste and flavors.
3. You can **add in** new ingredients but add them one at a time so you can tell what's been changed in the final resulting juice.

There are also some save-yourself-the-trouble guidelines that seem popular among juicers. These are tips on what *not* to mix together but again, you may be the exception that likes them. These are just tips:

1. Cantaloupe, watermelon and honeydew are great juiced by themselves but they do not mix well with vegetables or with each other. Cantaloupe with strawberry tastes delicious. Some fresh mint in the watermelon also works. Beyond that, proceed at your own risk!

2. Grapefruit does not mix well with tomato or beets.

3. Pears and tomatoes don't mix well.

4. Prune juice does not go well with cabbage or garlic.

5. Berries—blackberry, raspberry, blueberry—don't mix well with beet root.

6. Grapes and carrots don't mix too well.

7. Cabbage, watercress or turnip juice do not mix well with lemon, orange, or grapefruit.

8. Pomegranate is best by itself or with a little apple. Does not mix well with vegetables.

9. Daikon radish, onions, dandelions, watercress, Mustard Greens have tastes and flavors that are very strong and bitter. Juice them in advanced stages of your juicing and in small tiny quantities.

10. Apple mixes with just about everything and is your number one vegetable-juice base and sweetener.

11. Green tops from carrots and beets can be juiced and are highly nutritious but extremely bitter. Start small and only after you've been adjusting to vegetable juice tastes.

12. Go easy on hot peppers such as cayenne and jalapeño, and add these only after you are used to juices and want to spice things up.

These are just guidelines again based on my personal experience and research as well as the general feedback of my juicing community. You may stumble upon many more combinations that you won't like or some of the above that you *do*! That's the beauty of juicing: we all have a unique experience with it.

A few more quick golden rules that I highly encourage you to follow:

1. Don't dilute your juices with water or ice. Work on getting the ratios right from pure juice ingredients.
2. Don't ever heat your juices. Drink them cold or at the room temperature in which you make them.
3. Do not drink your juices along with a meal. Drink them on a relatively empty stomach and let your body absorb all the goodness then eat an hour or two afterwards.

So now you have the basic tools to add the art and the science to create your own recipes or modify existing ones. Enjoy!

JUICER IN THE SPOTLIGHT

Sue Mitchell, who loves creating her own recipes and continues to be surprised by the amazing benefits of juicing both on the inside and the outside.

"Honestly, the main reason I do green juicing is I love the juice! I wouldn't do this if I had to choke down some wretched concoction just because it was good for me. At the same time, I can really feel how good it is for me with every sip. Green juice gives me an energetic and satisfied feeling no other food can really match. Since I started drinking green juices, I feel much more energetic and in control of my life. My hair, nails and skin are noticeably healthier and I just feel stronger in every way. I'm making better choices in all areas of my life because I'm operating from a place of greater wellness. I never thought I'd give up caffeine, but I found I had so much energy from the juice that the caffeine buzz started to feel over the top. I still love coffee, so I've switched to decaf. The extra energy has also helped me be more consistent with my exercise routine. I've lost a few pounds in a gradual, steady way that feels like something I can sustain. Oh, and I also love experimenting. Like a mad scientist in the kitchen, I test out different recipes to find wonderful ways to nourish my body."

Pushing Past the Resistance to Keep Juicing

When you start a new healthy habit, the initial excitement is all you need to get going and to learn all the basics. But then something interesting starts to happen: you begin to hit tiny little bumps of inner resistance along the way and find yourself having a harder time doing the same thing you were excited about just weeks ago. What gives?

If or when you start to lose enthusiasm and shift into a different place than when you started. First, know that this is perfectly normal; we all go through the process of adapting to change. We go through this as it is our human nature to want to hold on to the old habits and routines to which we are so accustomed. Breaking free from a habit that your body and mind has built over the years takes time, but also subtle mental shifts of perspective. Without the latter, you will be starting new habits only to stop them a short while later. Sound familiar?

Juicing is no exception. It is a habit. It is a lifestyle. It is change that your whole body and mind system needs to embrace if—and only if—you want to make the habit stick. If you just want to try it for fun and do it once in a while when the mood strikes, you can skip this chapter. If you want to integrate juicing into your life, then this chapter is a must-read.

So how do you make the habit stick and push past the bumps of resistance? What are the signs and symptoms of the resistance in the first place so you can identify them right from the start? What are some practical ways you can deal with them right away? Dive into the chapter to find out and I'll see you there.

How to Keep That Initial Motivation Going Strong and Long

Motivation is what gets you started. Habit is what keeps you going.
~ Jim Ryan

One of the reasons we fall out of juicing is because of the time and effort juicing requires, and most of us do not have a personal chef that can respond to our every whim and wish. A lot of naysayers to juicing tell me that flat out: they don't want to get into it because it takes "so much time!" My argument is that so does having children but people keep having them because the reward is unquestionably worth it. The rewards of juicing are absolutely worth it, too.

The difference is that with children and babies, you feel a sense of urgency to tend to them or else. But your body cannot scream at you like a baby if you stop juicing—it would be nice if it did—instead, it sends subtle hints that most of us are conditioned to ignore. So most naysayers of juicing either never start or start and then soon talk themselves out of it at the first sign of resistance with the big fat excuse of *"but it takes so much time!"*

You are not a naysayer; I just wanted you to be wary of them. You are a winner at juicing and other health habits that you start. You are here to learn how to keep that initial motivation going strong

with understanding first, why it diminishes over time, second how to build it up for the long haul and third, how to create a system and methodology so that juicing does not take all that much time! How's that for a super agenda? Let's do it!

Why the Resistance?

When you do something good for your body or your mind, there is a process that you go through. You don't just switch on a light and go from your current state to the good healthy state. You will experience a lot of bad stuff first before the good prevails. But the good news is that the bad stuff has to come *up* to be released.

Just like cleaning your body, whether you are washing the outside or detoxing the inside with a juice fast, first the bad stuff has to come to the surface and be released and washed out before you can get to the squeaky clean state. The same is true with the thoughts and the mind. You are changing out the old ways of thinking and doing things with the new refreshing habits. The old stuff needs to come up to be *released* first before you can get to the ultimate state of joy and bliss.

The deeper and longer you go into your health habits, the more of the bad stuff you need to release first, but the better and firmer you also establish the new habit to make it stick around!

The resistance then comes up when all your old approaches to taking care of yourself clash with the new habit of juicing. There is no way for them to co-exist and so you have to choose. That's why it gets hard to move along swimmingly after the initial excitement has worn off because now you have to make some decisions: What stays and what goes?

Juicing is not a singular stand-alone habit. Juicing is a holistic lifestyle shift to health and vitality because it organically affects your other bad habits and makes it very hard to continue both. When you add juicing into your life, it just may not work well in combination with some of your existing habits.

Just like if you are a smoker and take up running, you experience a similar situation: You cannot do both for long and take full pleasure in either because they clash with each other. One gets to stay. The other must go. You decide which but first arm yourself with some knowledge on the signs of resistance.

What Are the Signs of Resistance?

As you go deeper and deeper into habits and making a change to the way that you do things and to the comfort zone that you are familiar with, you will start to feel resistance out of nowhere.

If you have been on a personal growth journey for a while, you may experience a milder level of resistance. If this is one of the first major health habits you are establishing, you'll have a higher level. How can you best prepare for it?

I classify two types of resistance; one comes from your physical body, your aches and pains and discomforts that the body exaggerates in order to have a firm excuse *not* to do something. The other is all in your head, the self-talk, the noise and chatter from your thoughts that give you lectures on what you can and cannot do, the worst and most effective form of self-sabotage.

So what are the more specific signs of resistance to watch for:
- You come up with random excuses that are fully justifiable to yourself.
- You use time as an excuse.
- You use money as an excuse.
- You use effort as yet another excuse.
- You use "just don't feel like it" excuse.
- You blame others—kids, spouse, friend, the pet—for getting in your way.
- You stop focusing on all the compelling reasons you initially started the habit.
- You call yourself unflattering names, such as weak, incapable, lazy, "not the sort of person that would do this."
- You tell yourself it was just a fun phase and not "practical" to make it a habit with your busy life.
- You find ways to cause mishap on purpose like messing things up or breaking things.

These are the loud and clear signs to watch out for but there can also be subtle and barely noticeable signs. Pay attention by slowing down and tuning in as to why you are resisting your juicing. Have a simple dialogue with yourself:

Why am I resisting juicing today?
What's getting in my way of juicing now?
What is the real reason I am not doing it?

The more clarity you can get around why your resistance is happening, the easier it is to break through it and push past it. It takes a lot of courage and honesty because this is not just about juicing. This could be about a lot of underlying issues and hang-ups you may have about healthy habits.

How to Push Past the Resistance to Juicing?

Now that you have identified the source of your resistance, let's learn how to outsmart it! Shall we? Here are four ways to gently push past the resistance to juicing:

1. Make the commitment to yourself loud and clear:

Have you made the commitment about juicing loud and clear to yourself and to everyone in your life that matters and may need to know of big changes in your health such as family, close friends and your primary physician? Making the verbal commitment to yourself crystal clear has an amazing effect on your actions. It brings your promise to light and reminds you that you are serious about this, and that you have every intention to make it happen. And it's easy to do! Just remind yourself and others verbally that you are committed to your juicing habit for the long-term.

2. **Create positive inner dialogue:**

The inner dialogue can be brutal. We are our own worst critic. If you listen to that chatter inside your head, it's the voice that tells you all the reasons you cannot do something and blames everything from your parents and upbringing to your current situation in life. You need to be the boss of that voice and not the other way around. Learn to silence it by reminding yourself that you are in control and that what it tells you simply isn't true.

It all stems from unfounded fear. I have felt this annoying fear and accompanying dialogues in my yoga journey and they held back my progress for years. My body would tense up and resist certain postures because it feared that I might "break" my body or experience deep pain, and tension is ironically when injury happens. The only way I have been able to go deep into those beautiful postures is by releasing these thoughts, breathing deeply and listening carefully to what the body is *really* trying to tell you amidst the mind chatter and all!

Learn to do this well and you can stick not just to your juicing but also to your many other health habits.

3. **Use the power of positive affirmations:**

If you have never done positive affirmations, start now. Positive affirmations are statements or mantras in the present-tense action verb, which you repeat over and over. This is a way to make your thoughts and your mind cooperate with your juicing habit rather than fight it. These affirmations will ease you into juicing with love instead of resistance. Here are a few but feel free to modify to make them your own:

- I release all my anxiety and doubt about juicing.
- I firmly believe juicing is great for my body and mind.
- I make juicing an integral part of my life.
- I have time and effort to dedicate to my juicing habit.
- I believe the time and effort is fully worth the rewards.
- Juicing is doing my body heaps of good.
- My body loves the juices even if it does not always show me right away.
- Juicing is a habit that brings me vitality and longevity.

Affirmations are fun and they work. Make up your own affirmations if these don't exactly speak to you. Then memorize them and repeat them to yourself. Write them on a sticky note and put them on your juicer or on the kitchen door or on your computer screen. Add these messages of encouragement especially in places where you tend to feel weak. Where are you at those times? What might you be looking at? This is your gentle effective way of pushing past the resistance, so be your own little

guardian angel to outsmart resistance. May juicing conquer all the resistance and doubt and bring you much bliss and good health.

A note on releasing all the anxiety and worry now that you are aware of it: The best technique is a form of physical exercise or activity that moves your body. Choose whatever form of activity that you enjoy! My number one choice is Ashtanga yoga. Yours can be anything you like, as long as it helps you release muscle tension and helps your mind get on board and, together, it gets you closer into a state of harmony.

4. **Prepare, plan and persist on your juicing:**

You are far more likely to juice if you set aside everything you need the night before and in fact, you might even feel a wee bit guilty if you don't juice after you have already prepared half the steps the night before. This is a great way to push past the resistance with a super practical approach. Here's how to do it:

- Get your juicer ready to go. Place it near the kitchen sink, plug it in and place the containers and the pusher for the chute on the counter.
- Take out your cutting board and knife.
- Put any strainers that you may use for washing your vegetables and fruits in the sink.
- Put your recipe out—either your physical recipe book or if it's a digital one, have it ready to pull out on your device.

- Get out your juice glass—either the one you drink at home or for on-the-go.
- Get out your glass containers if you will have leftovers to store in the fridge.
- Go to your fridge and set aside all your ingredients in a corner of the fridge so they are ready to grab.
- Put out any towels and cleaning supplies and brushes that you need for the washing and cleaning stage.

If you take all these steps the night before or a few hours prior to your juicing, it's a safe bet that you will be juicing when the time arrives!

Practice these ways of working through the resistance. It takes repetition to get them under control so be gentle but firm with yourself. What if you mess up? Well, keep reading as to why you need to forgive more often in this journey of juicing.

Juicing Is Human But Forgiveness Is Divine

In order to change we must be sick and tired of being sick and tired.
~ **Fannie Lou Hamer**

The only person that gets in our way to success and happiness is our own self. It's a truth we face on the path to self-discovery, and understanding this, instead of fighting it, can unlock our success at whatever it is we want to do. Let's learn to become our own best friend instead of acting as our own worst enemy, shall we?

First Decide, Then Act Accordingly

One of the best things to do at the very beginning of your juicing journey is consciously decide *how* you are going to react when you fall off the wagon, mess up, and just quit altogether for the time being. Instead of waiting for the inevitable to happen, just have a plan that helps you stay the captain of your ship instead of being at the mercy of the storm or the wind.

When I first started juicing in 2007, years of self-discipline in other areas of my life had hardened me. Sure, that good old discipline helped me accomplish great things over the years, but it was also a harsh approach to building habits. It failed miserably when I applied it to my juicing habit. Whenever I would miss even a day in my daily juicing commitment, which is a huge undertaking in itself, I would berate and punish myself. I would sabotage all the good efforts that I put in at the beginning with the brutal way that I reacted to my slip-ups on those rare occasions.

The result of those harsh reactions was *not* a more disciplined approach to juicing but more frequent and longer lapses. The more severely I reacted to myself for missing out on my juicing commitment, the less interested I became in the whole thing and soon, it wasn't fun anymore. My harsh reactions may have pulled me back on track a few times but they did not create any long-term results. In the end, I quit my promising juicing habit for a good part of 2008 until I learned a big lesson that helped me dive back into it in 2009 with an attitude and a mindset that has kept me going strong since then.

What happened? I changed my entire approach to lapses and built a sustainable habit that can not only survive but also thrive with the occasional demands of a busy life that weighs on all of us. Here's what I learned:

Why to Forgive Your Juicing Lapses

Juicing is human but forgiveness is divine.

If you can forgive yourself for missing a day or a week or longer when your life has other plans (beware that these are not some silly excuses as we discussed earlier so much as *real* urgencies that require your time and attention), it is going to serve you much better than any punishment or berating you could dish up!

Building a smart sustainable health habit is not easy, and when you fall out of it, you blame yourself but alas these feelings of guilt are the *last thing* you need. You should only concern yourself with one thing: how to *get back into the habit* as quickly as possible.

So you fall out. So you stop doing something you said you were going to do every day or every week. Big deal! It's done, it's over, it's behind you and today is all that you should focus on because that is the only thing you can control.

What will separate you from others when it comes to building the smart and sustainable habit of juicing is what you do after you fall out of the habit, because at some point, life happens to all of us and we get side-tracked. It is what we do *after* the lapse that makes all the difference.

Here are some practical ways to get back into your juicing habit after you fall off the wagon. Do these in order and pace yourself as you ramp back up:

1. **Forgive yourself completely.** Do not weigh yourself down with feelings of guilt and shame and blame. Treat this as an experiment with a bump in the road; you can fix the bump and the experiment is far from over. Forgive yourself fast so you don't

take away energy from the obvious, which is finding your way back to your regular juicing.

2. **Look back at what triggered the change** in your behavior to analyze what happened so that you prevent it from happening in the future. For instance, was it a change in your routine or lifestyle? Was it the start of traveling season, getting together with family, onset of social life, or other obligations? This can have a two-fold effect: It helps you forgive yourself much more easily and it allows you to plan better next time your life is headed in that direction.

3. **Aim to plan better in the future** once you know the root cause of what interrupted your habit. For instance, if you know you will be traveling, then plan to have a strong few weeks of green juicing building up to your trip and then locate a few juice bars at your destination if you can work them into your schedule. If you know that family will be visiting at your own home, consider doing your juicing while they are there and invite them to join you in on it. If you will be visiting family away from home, consider taking some juices in a cooler or pack up your juicer if you are traveling by car. The options are plenty once you start thinking with a solution-oriented mindset.

4. **Celebrate the successes of getting back into the habit.** It is really important that you reward yourself for taking such good care of your body and your health. Rewarding does not mean stuffing your face with chocolate cake and candy, dear heart! It

simply means thinking kindly of yourself, thanking yourself and acknowledging yourself for being such a champion. It means rewarding in a healthy way to reinforce further enhancing your overall well-being.

So next time you have a lapse, let it go and be forgiving and kind to your fabulous self. Then, put a plan in place to ease back into things with a gentle but firm resolve. Always come from an empowered place that says you can do this, you believe this is good for you and you are human, so having one lapse or even ten is fine as long as **you keep going**, and that you will do beautifully if you learn to forgive and to get right back on the juicing wagon!

Why a Juicing Journal Is Your Best Friend

Remembrance of things past is not necessarily the remembrance of things as they were.
~ Marcel Proust

When I started juicing in 2007, we had just come back from Tokyo where I had bought a lovely Japanese notebook that for months was "too beautiful" to use for anything, until one day I had the urge to document my juicing experience in it in great detail. I titled the notebook "My Grand Juicing Experience," picked up one of my best pens and started writing.

I am so glad I followed that instinct because a week after making a new recipe, I would have no idea whether I loved a recipe or if it turned out to be just OK or how much of what I put in it. You may have a better memory, but you won't be able to trust your memory alone about the growing details over time. In this juicing journal, I documented each new ingredient, each new recipe, the flavors and colors, my reaction to the juice at the time, my top likes and dislikes and how I felt after drinking it. They weren't just a collection of recipes. They were stories about each juicing experience. Later, when I started blogging and then writing newsletters on juicing and my first book, I had a stack of recipes with firsthand experience that I could share in detail. Even today, I reference the juicing journal occasionally.

Whether you have a physical or digital journal, one thing you can take advantage of is the ubiquitous camera phone that comes installed in almost all phones. Get used to taking pictures of your juicing process. A quick snapshot of all your ingredients laid out, cut up and ready to go, is going to be so helpful when you wonder how much of what you put in that recipe that tasted so good. Also, it gives you a visual journey of the various produce you are juicing, and if you wonder whether you've juiced too much or too little of something, it's really easy to scroll through your photos to quickly see. You can also take photos of your juice—the color, the foam, and the amount—and save a series of photos per recipe. You can organize all your juicing photos in an album to keep it apart from the rest of your pictures.

That's what I want to get you excited about today: Your very own juicing journal!

With every health habit, you have a choice. You can look at it as "something to do and get over and done with." Or you can look at it as a journey, an experience, a path that teaches you more about who you are, what your likes and tolerances are and how willing you are to explore new things and grow to become a better version of yourself in the process. Let your juicing be a *big deal* and treat it as such a journey.

How does a juicing journal work itself into experience? It sounds like a tall order but small things can have big effects and journeys are best when they are documented! In a way, you re-live the experience by writing even your shortest account on each part of the journey, and you emphasize to yourself the fact that you are doing so much good to your body. That is the essence of keeping a juicing journal; it is a way to build this habit deep into your system and to help you return to it in the future, when and if you have lapses along the way.

That is the *most* important reason. Here are seven more ways you will benefit from keeping a juicing journal:

1. **Remember your most favorite recipes exactly**—not just "sort of!" Imagine, a few weeks or months down the road, you'll know exactly what recipe made you salivate! Remember that awesome most delicious combination of flavors to be able to easily repeat later or know exactly what needed modification if you wrote down: too sweet, too sour, too pungent, use less of this and more of that.

2. **Show visible progress in your juicing journey**, both in terms of frequency and developing your taste buds. This goes a long way in keeping you motivated when you can see your progress on paper. It shows you the effort you have put in, the milestones you have covered, the new things you have tried. It is your own quick motivation booster!

3. **Know which combination of flavors worked or did not work**. There will be tastes—singular or combinations—that your body will not like, and you want to remember that. This way, you

will have a nice reference of which juices caused your body a less-than-great reaction, what happened, how long it lasted and if you are willing to try it again or set it aside for now.

4. **Keep tabs on your total body reaction.** Each of us reacts differently and even you may even have different reactions to the same juice at different times. But I have found that sometimes, there are patterns and it's nice to recognize them. For instance, beet juice is an excellent eliminator for me, and green juice with pineapple as a base sweetener is a delicious filler and "happy" drink for me. Document which juices give you results in terms of elimination, hydration and filler, curbing cravings or energy boosting.

5. **Mark the gaps in your juicing journey and speculate on the reasons** such as the change in seasons, the weather, travel, moodiness and other factors. Let's face it, we are human and we are going to have ups and downs in our habits, no matter how well grained they may be. The way to come out on top is to keep pushing through, and that you can do with the help of your journal by learning what got in the way. If you had a lapse of two weeks, just make a note of it in your journal. If you didn't feel like juicing or you weren't in the vicinity of a juicer or a juice bar, what-ever your life events may be, journal it and find your way back to it by your next journal entry.

6. **Have a record of your emotional ups and downs where notable**; this is especially useful during a juice fast of any length.

If you are juicing extensively or going on any type of a juice fast or a different kind of deep detox, it is a drastic change from the norm, so document your emotional ups and downs: anxiety, stress, sadness, unhappiness, moodiness, grumpiness, calmness, clarity and everything in between. This is especially useful as you do multiple fasts and detoxes to see progress over time or to avoid certain pitfalls if you know what caused them.

7. **Be able to share your best recipes with friends and family and others who are interested**. This is one of the best reasons because people will ask you about recipes more than you can imagine, and having it written down or typed up is a great way to access it quickly. Not only is the juicing journal a fabulous reference for yourself, it is also incredibly useful when the outside world wants to know your best kept juicing secrets, assuming you are willing to share them!

Your juicing journal does not have to be a notebook from the Far East, or even a physical notebook for that matter. You can use anything you like, or if you prefer to have a digital version, you can use a computer file or the Evernote application or another system to keep track of your experience. Use a method that you enjoy and one that you can keep up with anytime anywhere. If you only have a journal on your main stationery computer, you may be less likely to remember to document it if you can't get to it right away. Mobile devices are great if you can use an app on your smartphone.

Remember: Make it fun! Make it easy! And make it a regular habit to document things right after before you forget the juicy details!

JUICER IN THE SPOTLIGHT

Rick Sidley, who started juicing at 68 and has become an avid fan of juicing.

"I came to juicing by accident, really. My wife Karin has been fighting esophageal cancer for two years now. She went through chemo then had a period of extreme pain due to a blood clot in her right kidney. The pain was the reason I jumped to finding out about green juicing. I read Farnoosh's first juicing book, and reread it, taking notes. I decided to take the plunge, for Karin, and as it has turned out, for myself. Through green juicing I am helping her make it day to day through this life battle. I can only say, do this if this is something you really want to make a part of your life, your routine, and your way of living. It is not easy as it does take a commitment but only two months later, I'm deep into the clear, blue water of this wonderful, pure, clear, green sea! Never thought it would be this good and it can only get better."

Upping the Ante: Juice Fasting, Baby!

In July of 2009, I embarked on my first five-day juice fast challenge. It was an extremely difficult commitment because I simply love to eat. I stay active so I like to nibble and snack constantly, and even if it's mostly healthy, it is much more than nourishment. It is my comfort and my friend. I enjoy my foods a lot and to give up eating for any length of time sounded like complete torture, and to give it up intentionally sounded nothing short of crazy. Alas, my curiosity got the best of me and off I went on my first juice fast.

When you start on a health journey, sometimes you find something that is an ideal match for your body and even your personality, and sometimes the total opposite. I believe that decisions about our health affect us as much on mental and psychological levels as they do on physical levels.

It is important to define the right reasons before you embark on your fast. For my first fast, I wanted to face—and overcome—the unnatural fear of giving up food. I had been terrified of the idea and wanted to test my own boundaries.

Now every time I do a juice fast, the experience gets easier. Like most habits, it makes me wonder why I don't do it more often! I hope you can feel this way after you have experienced the delights of juice fasting. After you become familiar with juicing, you start having fun with it because not only is it good for you but also because you start to crave and love it. That's when you are ready to up the ante by experimenting with juice fasts.

Fresh juices are meant to supplement a balanced diet and not replace it. Juice fasting is the exception to this rule. When you are on a juice fast, you replace your diet with fresh juices for a period of time and give your digestive system a rest. Juice fasts are an ideal way to cleanse and detox your system, but it's also one of the more nebulous aspects of juicing, so having a set of guidelines can be helpful.

In this chapter, we talk about the essentials of a juice fast, what juice fasting is and how to go on a juice fast, how to listen to your body and how to start and break the fast, and what to expect while fasting. Ready to get started?

One word of caution: Before you start your first fast, please check with your doctor. As much as I like to make my own decisions, I too checked with my primary physician before my five-day and ten-day juice fasts. In fact, in *Fat, Sick and Nearly Dead*, a fantastic documentary by Joe Cross that I have dubbed as the "must-watch film of every juice lover," Joe checks in with his doctor in Australia every step of the way as he completes his 60 (yes 60!) day juice fast.

And one more thing: Juice fasting is a lot of work. I have done several juice fasts ranging in length from 24 hours to ten days.

I spent an hour to two hours in the kitchen every day preparing the juices, so don't plan your fast for a crazy busy time in your schedule. This is a big commitment and you need to be prepared to see it through, but with the amazing way you will be feeling on the fast, you will enjoy every bit of the work!

So get ready to learn about juice fasts, grab a glass of juice, take a comfortable seat and dive into the chapter. I'll see you there.

What Is Juice Fasting and Why Do It?

He that eats till he is sick must fast till he is well.
~ **English proverb**

Juice fasting means you abstain from all solid foods, including raw fruits and vegetables and even the extra pulp that your juicer may dispense along with the juice. Why? Because the main goal of a juice fast is to give your digestive system a complete rest, so anything that needs the help of your digestive organs is off-limits. This also includes chewing gum, which activates the digestive system with the simple act of chewing, even if you produce nothing but saliva in the process.

Besides a ban on solid foods, you should also abstain from alcohol, smoking, sodas and bottled drinks during a fast.

Now, the two negotiable exceptions are coffee and tea. The question to help you decide the answer is this: How much of a cleanse do you want with a juice fast? In the strictest juice fast guidelines, giving up caffeine (in coffee) and theine (in tea) is necessary because your body can cleanse and purify easier without the interference of these stimulants. That's all well and good but if giving up your black cup of coffee or green tea gives you massive headaches and makes you impossibly moody, I say go easy at least on your first fast and leave it in.

I tend to make one exception for myself: tea. I choose not to go without my loose-leaf Oolong tea. I do not drink coffee anymore but tea can have exceptional health qualities. Plus, I have found that the combination of juicing and hot tea during a fast is total bliss for my body. It helps elimination of waste; it keeps me warm because juicing alone without solid foods can make your body temperature drop, and it helps me stay productive. And drinking tea—as well as black coffee—does not activate your digestive system so the main purpose of fasting remains intact. For me, giving up my tea during a fast would be too disruptive to the flow of life and the benefits are not worth the trade-off.

You can get immense benefits from fasting while making an exception for some unadulterated coffee or tea in between your juices. Hold the cream and sugar, please! And if you want to do without your coffee and tea, then have some hot water with fresh-squeezed lemon juice for an ideal hot drink. If you want to get adventurous, you can add some fresh ginger juice and/or garlic juice into your hot water and lemon and make it pure medicine in a cup!

What about adding protein powder to your juices during the fast? I get this question a lot and the answer is no. I do not add anything to my fresh juices, fasting or not. The idea is to stay natural—supplements are not from Mother Nature exactly—and you're fasting to detox your body, not to gain muscle or build strength. You are fasting to clean out your digestive system and give your body and mind a complete rest. Supplements have no business in your system during a regular short-term (three to ten day) fast. Besides, I hate for you to mess with the natural taste and texture of the juice itself.

Also, I am not recommending that you stop or continue taking your regular medication one way or another. I am not a doctor. If you are on medication and want to go on a fast, please check with your doctor first.

If you happen to go on a long fast such as a 30-day fast or the super long 60-day fasts like my friend Israel Torres, you can choose to take some essential supplements such as Omega 3-6-9, folic acid and other minerals and supplements to fill in the gaps on the long-term fast. Again, feel free to check with your doctor or nutritionist in this regard.

After years of experimenting with foods and diets and health habits, I can tell you that there is no hard and fast rule on how to do something. There are only guidelines and best practices on how to do a beneficial fast. You are not breaking the law here if you need to modify slightly, and besides, you need to be able to have some fun as you push yourself in the right direction. Remember to make the right modifications for you, and be less stressed and more excited about the whole prospect of fasting, alright?

To recapture the way to get best results from juice fasting, here's what you give up:

- Solid foods
- Sodas
- Bottled drinks
- Alcohol
- Gum
- Smoking

And what you take in during a fast:
- Fresh juices without pulp
- Filtered room-temperature water
- Hot water and lemon
- If desired, moderate amounts of black coffee or tea

Now that you have an idea about the "what" of juice fasting, let's talk about the bigger question: "Why." Fasting is a big commitment and it's easy to see your motivation wane and find yourself wondering why you are even bothering. Knowing **your big why** will keep you grounded when your mind gets weak.

As you read each of the ten benefits below, ask yourself if that particular benefit is important to you. Just because juice fasting can give you a certain benefit doesn't mean *you* can get all excited about it. We do things for our own reasons and I want you to find out what that reason is for you, because a juice fast works best when you are doing it for the motive that makes sense to you, not to me or to some health expert out there.

So in the list below, find your main motive—you may have more than one—and then lock yourself into it. Then remind yourself constantly that is why you are embarking on your juice fast.

Top ten benefits of juice fasting:

1. A juice fast gives your digestive system a much-needed break.
2. A juice fast helps you calm your mind and quiet your nervous system.
3. A juice fast is a good way to lose the stubborn weight in a safe way.
4. A juice fast helps to cleanse and detox your internal organs.

5. A juice fast can expedite the elimination and flushing out of accumulated body waste.
6. A juice fast can give you time to reflect on your diet and your lifestyle and reset the switch on it all.
7. A juice fast enhances the benefits of concurrent bodywork such as yoga, meditation or massage.
8. A juice fast clears your skin and releases toxins from the colon, kidneys, bladder, lungs and sinuses.
9. A juice fast can make you reflect on life and help expedite healing.
10. A juice fast gives you a surprising amount of energy and clarity.

For me, my motives for fasting have changed over time. With my first juice fast, I was just curious to experience the sensation of giving up food for a few days. For the next juice fast, I wanted to drop a few stubborn pounds now that I had conquered the initial fears of fasting. For my ten-day juice fast, I wanted to go into that heightened state of awareness and clarity and channel the extra energy into writing and a daily meditation practice. And for my last three-day juice fast, I was a fast buddy to my husband on his very first juice fast.

All my fasts were blissful experiences despite the initial bouts of hunger and possible crankiness. After you get over that first hump, which is the first two or three days, you will begin to feel really good.

So what is the driving force that will make you want to say: "I want to go on a juice fast now!" Find it and keep it on the forefront of your mind as you plan for your first exciting juice fast.

I saw few die of hunger; of eating, a hundred thousand.
~ Benjamin Franklin

Easing into It: Prepare for Your First Fast

*From the bitterness of disease man learns the
sweetness of health.*
~ Catalan Proverb

A juice fast can be a tremendous shift toward a healthier, happier you. We talked about the benefits of juice fasting and how to go on one, so if you are still here, you mean business. Wonderful! Now let's talk about some of the challenges with juice fasting so you are not caught off-guard for your first fast.

First, if you do not feel committed to the labor involved in planning, purchasing, washing, cutting and preparing your juices, as well as cleaning up the mess after the fact, juice fasting on your own is out of the question.

The main challenge on the mind of a juice fast newbie is how to keep hunger at bay, but don't overlook the daily preparation efforts that go into making your fresh juices. You may be able to buy them if you live close to a juice bar, but it would be a limited selection and much more expensive and you would need large doses of juice because that's your "meal" during a fast.

The only other option for you is to find a juice-delivery service. I know some large cities such as New York City and places in California offer this. You can even sign up for a juice fast program.

But you are more than likely doing it on your own so let's get you good and ready for it!

The Downsides of a Fast:

The time and effort investment is one of the down sides of the juice fast. I will give you a few other precautions to keep in mind and I do this not to intimidate you one bit. Just to inform you. When you know what's coming, you can handle it with poise and grace, so here goes:

1. **A juice fast is not easy.** You need to be mentally and psychologically prepared for abstaining from food. I repeat, this is not easy and anyone who tells you otherwise is lying. The first 24 to 48 hours are the hardest. Then your body slowly enters a state where it moves beyond hunger and you start to feel more relaxed. The latter stages of a fast are ironically easier from a hunger standpoint.

2. **A juice fast may make you very emotional.** The emotions rising to the surface are a part of the healing process but the fast can still make you moody, cranky and easily annoyed and maybe even slightly depressed if you do not take good care of yourself. You can counteract this by preparing for it, thinking positive thoughts, taking naps and baths and getting massages, curling up with a book, telling yourself that it's perfectly normal to feel this way, keeping stressful work to a minimum and letting your

loved ones know so that they can be extra supportive during this period.

3. **A juice fast may be disruptive to your social life** so plan accordingly. Your fast is for a limited period and probably a short one if you are just starting out, but the last thing you need is peer pressure from family, friends or colleagues—even if they all mean well or are just teasing you—so if possible, abstain from social events or be forthcoming about your fast and drink your juice before attending the event so you do not get tempted to eat or drink while there.

4. **A juice fast is non-forgiving**, so that means if you slip and eat during the fast, your fast is over and you need to start again. You don't need to get upset with yourself but when your digestive system starts to work again, you need to end and re-start the fast. So be careful because you may naturally forget that you are fasting and end up putting something in your mouth! It helps to have no food around and to remind yourself that you are fasting as you make your juices, so you don't nibble on the raw veggies before they go down the juicer's chute!

5. **A juice fast takes a lot of work and preparation**. You need to plan in advance, and accept that you will be doing this work during a fast when you may not be particularly upbeat or full of energy. You need to do the shopping, cleaning, storing away the produce, and making your juices. You need to have your system

down pat and be as efficient and organized about it as possible to keep yourself motivated.

6. **A juice fast is relatively costly**: You already have a juicer of course if you are juicing. You will be juicing a lot of fresh fruits and vegetables and not using the pulp during this time. It can be a wee bit costly. You can cut this cost by shopping at your local grocery store instead of Whole Foods or Farmer's Market, planning really well so nothing goes to waste, buying local or regular instead of organic, which is usually cheaper and sometimes just as good, and sticking to less expensive fruit and vegetable options or planning your recipes around the produce that is on sale.

7. **A juice fast can be hard to do if you are physically active.** If you maintain a vigorous exercise program or a crazy work and social life schedule, tone it down during your fast. Try to do the fast in a quieter time and with the ability to rest and relax often. You can still go on walks, do your stretches and have a medium aerobic activity, but remember to use this time to take a break from hyperactivity, both on your digestive system and on the physical exercise levels.

The good news is this. For all my own juice fasts as well as everyone else that I have coached, worked with in my juicing clinic or interviewed on the subject: A juice fast is most definitely worth it!

The Length of the Fast:

Now that you are mentally ready, let's talk about how long you should fast for? Again, this is where you need to check in with your doctor and make sure fasting is safe for you. If you have never fasted, I would suggest you go on a 24-hour to 48-hour juice fast first. Do this to get your body used to the idea of giving up food and consuming juices in larger quantities than just the occasional glass or so a day that you might be having. This also gives you confidence that you can indeed do this!

After your first short fast, take a couple of weeks to get back to a normal eating cycle and then plan for a longer fast. I have found the five-day fasts to be ideal length as a beginner. There is no magic behind the number five; I chose it because it is *just* long enough to help you experience the deeper benefits of fasting.

During this period of time, your body has time to first go through the initial bouts of hunger from mild to severe in the first 24–48 hours. Then it can quietly enter the detox zone where it cleanses your system and lets your digestive organs rest.

I also found five days to be a number that I could mentally digest especially since I had to overcome irrational fears of my temporary detachment from food. Anything more than five days seemed impossible in my mind and anything shorter would have not given me any benefits worth noting.

Whether you do two days, five days or nine days, make sure that you decide the length *before* you start your juice fast. It is much easier to stay with what you initially tell yourself you will do. On my 10 day juice fast with a friend from my juicing clinic, we set out to just "fast as long as we can" and we did not have a set goal. We had said "maybe two weeks, maybe longer," but it was a very loose target, and instead of giving us freedom to explore, it played to our disadvantage. Every time we felt weak or emotional, we would wonder if we had fasted long enough and if we should just break it. If we had a set target, we would not have entertained those conversations at all. Set your juice fast length before you start and stick to it as much as possible. It does wonders for your mind and your confidence!

How to Listen to Your Body During the Fast:

I also want to encourage you to tune in and listen to your body and honor your needs and mental state to help you choose the right duration of fast. Listening to your body is a heightened sense of awareness that you can develop over time. I use the phrase "listen to your body" a lot and here's how I define it.

1. Be actively in tune with your body and regularly check in with yourself, as you would check on your pet for instance. Ask yourself: How is my body feeling? What is the current state of everything? How is my energy level? How is my mood? How is my body reacting to this new juice or this new recipe?

2. Honor symptoms such as any pain, nausea, headache, stomachache, light-headedness or other physical signs of discomfort as soon as you feel them by taking rest and reducing stress and hyperactivity. If you are fasting during the winter, you may also get very cold; socks, staying indoors and hot tea or hot water and lemon helps a lot. Slow down or adjust the pace of your activities until you feel better. If things do not improve after a couple of hours, then stop your fast and slowly come out of it.

3. Learn to distinguish between the above and the inner chatter that says you can't do something or you are too weak or too old or too out of shape to do this. It is a voice that talks down to you and creates a false sense of fear and anxiety if you give it a lot of power. That's your ego talking, not your body, and that's a voice that you are free to ignore!

The Timing of the Fast:

The best preparation is listening to your body not just during a fast or with juicing, but all the time. Now let's talk about what other preparations you can make.

First, *time* your fast well. Do your fast at a time when you can be home, near your juicer and with access to a grocery store, possibly even a Farmer's Market, Indian or Asian grocery store or a place where you can get some more exotic vegetables, herbs and fruits that your regular grocery store may not carry. Do the fast at a time that does not coincide with stressful situations

at your work (i.e. before a huge deadline or presentation), any medical procedures and outside your menstrual cycle if you are a female.

If you can do your fast in the spring, the summer or the warm part of fall, it is easier on your system than if you do it in the cold of winter. Also, make sure you are feeling good before embarking on your fast. Don't do the fast if you are just coming off a cold or have been sick and feel weak still from its effects.

And last but not least, it's best if you can minimize your social activities as well as your intense physical activities or training for a big physical event like a marathon.

Getting Ready to Start the Fast:

Now you are ready to go on your fast. If you are doing a fast longer than 48 days, then you want to give your body a head start. If you are reading this book, you are a health-conscious eater (or at least you are on your way there). Two to three days before you start your fast, kick your healthy eating habit into high gear. Ideally, remove all meats and dairy from your diet three days before the fast, longer if you can, and eat lots of raw fruits and vegetables. Eating raw will help your body get ready for the fast and ease you into it by helping you give up food in stages. You can add some raw nuts and some light vegan soups into the mix. Eat this way until you start your fast.

As you get ready for the fast, it's critical to be in a positive mental state. You can do this, and you are stronger and more resilient than you think. One thing that works brilliantly is positive affirmations, which are mantras or encouraging phrases that you repeat to yourself before and during your fast. Of course, it helps to *really* believe them! They help you get in the right frame of mind and they remind you that you are capable of doing whatever you set your mind to.

Here are a few of my favorites, feel free to steal them away or make up some of your own:

1. I am healthy and strong and can do this fast.
2. I am nourishing and healing my body with natural juices.
3. I am doing this fast to reset, restart and revive myself.
4. I am discovering my own patience and boundaries in this fast.
5. I am restoring my body to its original state of health and vitality.

Are you now ready to start your fast experience now?

I can tell you that this experience is always a net gain and the detachment process is a beautiful step into understanding yourself. And a deeper understanding of ourselves opens us to a richer and happier life.

When you practice food detachment by fasting, you take a deep journey into understanding your body, your limits, your patience, your reaction to going without food, your resilience and so much more. Because attachment is so fundamental to our happiness, and so psychologically integrated into our nervous system, you get to know yourself on an intimate level during the fasting process. That knowledge brings you closer to your true self. When you have this level of knowledge, you can make smart decisions about the right approach to health that works well for your body and your lifestyle. So the benefits of the fast continue long after the fast is over, you see?

You also find out that you can temporarily survive just fine without solid food. You realize that humans do indeed survive without eating for a long period of time as long as they stay hydrated. This information opens your eyes to a new world and offers you a new perspective on food.

During my second and third fasts, I was mostly looking for a way to quiet my mind and to practice surrender to my attachments in life. And I did. During the fast, my mental energy shifted focus and the unimportant stuff just fell by the wayside; I crave to have that feeling again.

I also wanted to fast so I could experience the changes of body and mind through an age-old health habit that is centuries and generations old, that of fasting. We are doing a special type of fasting with juices, but the idea of fasting has withstood the test of time for as long as humans have been around.

Whatever your goals and desires may be from fasting, may the experience be so remarkable that you want to do it again and may it bring you closer to a better, happier version of yourself.

Eat little, sleep sound.
~ Iranian proverb

The Guidelines for Best Juice Fast Results

He who has health has hope, and he who has hope has everything.
~ A Proverb

Now that you are ready to dive into your juice fast experience, let's talk about how you can make this a great experience that you want to repeat regularly. What do you need to do to get the best results from your juice fast?

During the few days prior to your fast, get pumped up about your upcoming adventure. Yes, it is an adventure and the only person that decides that is *you!* Make it a fun one! Get your juicer and all your jars out, clean them out and set them on the counter in an accessible place, preferably close to the kitchen sink. If other things have to go back in the cupboards or cabinets for the duration of the fast, then so be it! Decide on glasses or plastic cups that you will be using to drink your juices, either while at home or to take to work with you. Make everything as ready to go as possible.

If you can, clean out the fridge and the pantry as much as possible from other foods and leftovers, and ban cooking in the kitchen if your lifestyle and family allow it. Smelling food during the fast is a big temptation that is best avoided. If you surround yourself with nothing but juices, you are less likely to think about food and be tempted. So make your environment as fast friendly as possible.

Planning Out Your Fast Recipes:

Then have fun planning out the recipes you will be making each day of your fast and, accordingly, prepare your shopping list for each day. Remember, it's OK if you don't stick to the recipes of each day. You want to leave some room for spontaneity, but on days when you have no idea what to make and you don't want to make a decision, making these plans in advance will come in handy.

The best way to plan out the recipes is to plan for two types of juices a day. Use your juicing journal to document your plans. If you make at least three to four batches for each recipe, then your days may look like this for a five-day juice fast:

Day 1, Recipe 1, Recipe 2.
Day 2, Recipe 3, plus Day 1 leftovers Recipes 1 and 2.
Day 3, Recipe 4 and leftovers from Recipe 3.
Day 4, Recipe 5 and 6 with leftovers from Recipe 4.
Day 5, Recipe 7, with Recipes 5 and 6 leftovers.

This way, you have rolling leftovers if you will, with at least two varieties of juice in the fridge at any given time. This works well if you have a masticating juicer because the juice from the centrifugal juicer doesn't store well. So if you have one of those, you will

be juicing twice a day, but it's a much faster turnaround with that machine.

You can start your mornings with a juice that has more fruit, such as a citrus-based juice, and make a more green juice for your lunch and dinner "meals." Just make sure that your recipes are different enough to give you as much variety in the fruits, vegetables and herbs as you can afford. For instance, if you make a fruit juice recipe, then make fruit and vegetable blend juice for the next recipe followed with vegetable juice for the following recipe. Aim to have no more than 15–20 percent fruit juice recipes and at least 50 percent highly green juice recipes. I consider the 100 percent fruit juices as my "desserts" during a fast and would have a small glass of it after the main green juice recipe for lunch or dinner. Yum!

Planning the Juicing Schedule:

It would be ideal to juice daily, and drink fresh juices for each "meal" of your fast, but that may not be practical for you. During my fasts, I tend to *want* to juice daily because it almost gives me something to do, I crave the fresh juice coming out of the juicer a lot during my fast and I feel engaged in the preparing of my "meal," but it's exhausting. You can make juices keep for 24–36 hours with a masticating juicer if you are extremely busy during your fast.

Whether you juice daily or every other day, prepare to set aside some time and effort when you won't be rushed or stressed. This means you may have to adjust some of your activities to accommodate the fast preparations. The time I spent in buying, washing, cutting, juicing and cleaning-up was about one to one and a half hours. This was when I used my masticating juicer that is slower than a centrifugal one. I calculated about seven to eight hours total time in preparation for the 5-day juice fast. I consider every second worthwhile because I did not want to take a shortcut and I didn't have access to a juice bar. You need to make the right decision for you.

During my first five-day juice fast, the recipes I used yielded 125 to 150 ounces (approximately one gallon) of juice. I bought organic for about 80 percent of my vegetables, simply for either availability at the time and my own measure of freshness between organic and standard produce. I prefer the leafy greens to always be organic.

The preparation phase was not all labor; I really did have fun with it and I think you will, too. A five-day juice fast is a huge commitment the first time, but I got better at it the second time and I would say the ten-day commitment was the easiest one of all. It's counter-intuitive but it shows that you do get better at it with practice, so don't get discouraged if the first fast is time-consuming, slow or challenging. You are doing your body an amazing good and should be proud of yourself!

How much juice should you consume during a fast and when should you drink? Because I was not interested in losing weight, I did not limit myself to how much juice I should drink per day except for the fruit juices. I would say be more conservative on your purely fruit juices and keep it to no more than one glass a day, but no limit on your green juices. If you are hungry, drink up. It does not have to be a set time of the day. If you are just bored or restless, however, watch out and try to do something else first—take a walk, take a nap, meditate, read, make a cup of tea or drink some water. Drink when you are hungry or low on energy—most people who fast do not drink enough juice and wonder why they are hungry. Drinking your juices will satiate your hunger, but just as you would with food, fight the urge to drink juice as a response to emotional highs and lows.

What to Expect During the Fast:

You can expect hunger in the first 24–48 hours of the fast, but this will go away. As unbelievable as it sounds, your stomach will stop growling and quiet down after day two. Remember, you may get emotional and extra-sensitive during the later stages of a fast but your hunger will subside.

On days 3 or 4, you may notice an increased sense of clarity and energy. This is a surprise to first-time fasters because it is so counter-intuitive. Indulge in it but don't go outside and run ten miles, because even though your energy is higher, your stamina may not be at its best. I would stay away from vigorous exercise at least on your first fast and instead enjoy the increase in productivity, take advantage of this clarity and focus on your important projects and tasks.

I remember going on a writing frenzy during my second five-day juice fast and wrote thousands of words. I was also not in the mood to socialize much, which was the perfect excuse to stay home and write, write and then write some more. The clarity, the flow of the words and the energy was unusual and most welcome! Just imagine what you could accomplish if the surge of energy comes to you during the fast.

And it's also possible that you may not have the surge of energy and that you may have a quieter experience during your fast. That's fine, too. Each fast is different so remember that your first fast experience does not dictate the future ones. My first five-day juice fast was one of the most difficult challenges I have ever taken on, and my ten-day juice fast, one of the most pleasant and fun challenges. So go along for the ride, and enjoy the unexpected surprises!

Your sleep patterns may be disrupted too. I've done several fasts and on about half of those fasts, my sleep schedule was interrupted. I was sleeping in smaller and more frequent chunks, so waking up earlier and maybe taking an afternoon nap. If you have the flexibility, go with the flow. If not, just beware of what's happening and accommodate yourself as best as you can.

To make your fast experience even more perfect, you may want to add other activities to your daily schedule that go extremely well with fasting. Any type of body work can do wonders for you during the fast. This includes but isn't limited to massages of all types, yoga, pranayama (breathing techniques from yoga), dry brushing your skin to stimulate lymph nodes for detox and baths with Epsom salts and/or essential oils. I also love to burn candles and incense during this time as well as read and meditate a lot.

You will notice that your senses will be in higher state of awareness during your fast. You will smell better, taste better, sleep more soundly and deeply when you do even if you go into different sleep patterns, and be far more alert and focused during the day. That's why your body will respond so much better to the body work during the fast, and together with the fast, it will help your body to detox and eliminate the built-up of waste over the years and to clean out your system from the inside out. You will be a whole new person after the fast.

Breaking Your Fast and Beyond

We never repent of having eaten too little.
~ Thomas Jefferson

Believe it or not, breaking the fast is the *most* challenging part of the whole experience. Be very careful how you break your juice fast. I did not give this one much thought during my first fast. I had focused on preparing and doing the fast itself and breaking it was just an afterthought. I will open my mouth and put some highly-anticipated solid food in it when the fast is over, thank you very much! That was the extent of my plan for breaking the fast.

What followed was a series of stomach pains, headaches and an awful and irritable mood that lasted 24 to 48 hours long. Now I have learned how to do this better but breaking the fast was the most difficult part of my first juice fast, which is why I have dedicated an entire section just on this topic.

For my second fast, I broke it gently with four to five small bites of banana that I chewed slowly and carefully with some water. Then I followed that in half an hour with a few spoonfuls from a ripe avocado, and an hour later, with one glass of watermelon juice. That was it for the rest of that first evening, followed by a similarly gentle breakfast, some fruit—banana, apple and strawberry—and some more juice. At the end of my ten-day juice fast, I was craving soup, so my husband made me a simple vegan soup—celery, carrots, oregano, spinach, onions and rice—and I had that with a few bites of avocado, one of my favorite foods on earth! In both of those fasts, I was able to ease back into eating with the better planning and judgment on the type and amount of foods to consume immediately after the fast.

How to Break Your Juice Fast:

Your stomach is slowly waking up from its slumber and the gentler, the slower and the easier you get back on solid foods, the better your overall experience shall be. I have listed some suggestions below on how you can break your fast:

1. **Decide on the time of day to break it in advance.** It's better to break the fast during the evening hours, that way you get one small portion of solid foods in your system and then go to sleep for a few hours before the next one.

2. **Prepare your breaking-the-fast food** and stay on a schedule so you don't get tempted to eat just everything in sight because you are no longer fasting. There are always exceptions, and one of them is my friend Israel Torres who after his 60-day juice fast walked into his favorite fast-food restaurant to have a fish sandwich! His juicing community was betting that he would end up in the hospital but he did just fine. He had a small portion and to his

credit, he did chew it very carefully! Israel's story is true but just for your amusement. Do not repeat this at home! Break that fast gently!

3. **Some options on how to break the fast:**
- A simple vegan soup
- Vegetable broth
- Fruit: banana, apple, pineapple, watermelon
- Vegetable: avocado, lettuce, spinach, kale, with a dollop of olive oil

4. **Foods to avoid for the first 48 hours after breaking the fast and longer if you can help it:**
- Fried foods
- Fast foods
- Foods made with heavy sauces
- Meats and fish
- Dairy products
- Spicy food
- Packaged foods

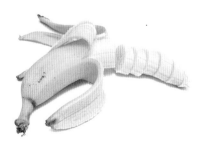

If you are still excited about doing a juice fast, I am excited for you. You must be ready! Remember that the juice fast is an excellent time to reflect on your eating habits, your lifestyle and even your life. Take the time to honor and understand the emotions you will experience, and learn to listen and get to know your body better. Since you are making such a tremendous commitment, be determined to reap all the benefits that you can.

Beyond the Juice Fast:

Once in a while, it is necessary to temporarily strip ourselves of the daily comforts if only to mark the edge of our strength and redefine the outer limits of our patience. When we do this, we give our internal system a rude awakening. Fasting is a return to the basics. It is a redefinition of what really matters. It is both a physical and a mental challenge and it shifts your perspective and reminds you why you should appreciate and therefore never abuse the abundance that is in your life.

In this case, that abundance refers to food, and a juice fast helps you understand your relationship with food and rebuild it the right way all over again. This level of experience and information can and will benefit you a thousand times over in every other area of your life. My juice fasts have taught me much about my body's endurance and resilience and patience.

Detaching yourself from things that seem indispensable in life is a funny process with an element of surprise. For instance, have you ever practiced material detachment, surviving without your material possessions for a period of time, be it by giving them away or by setting them aside for a while and not using them? You learn immediately that you really *can* survive and do just fine without a lot of "stuff." There is a difference between choosing to have something versus needing it. That's true both for the material world and the food world and fasting is a way to learn your body's real needs.

My buddy Israel Torres who admits that he has never led a healthy lifestyle, started juice fasting soon after watching *Fat, Sick and Nearly Dead* by Joe Cross. At the time of this writing, he was on his fourth 60-day juice fast, had lost over 100 pounds and had never felt better. He has shocked himself and everyone he knows with his determination to return to total health with his long and hard juice fasts. He is healthier, happier and no longer carries all that extra weight and pressure around. Israel is truly an inspiration when it comes to fasting. He has pushed the limits even far beyond Joe Cross himself and he did not start out as a health champion. He was a regular guy and weighed over 280 pounds and is now a fit, happy and super healthy guy. What limits can you blow out of the water in your own journey to health?

As long as you experiment safely and carefully, always keeping your well-being in mind and never risking harm to your body by forcing yourself into anything, you can reap huge benefits from a juice fast. I recommend strongly that you do consult your primary physician, or someone who knows your medical history and is familiar with your health records, to let them know you will be going on a fast and see if there may be any concerns. I share with you only the extent of my knowledge, research and experience and encourage you to make the best and most informed decision for yourself. I wish you the very best on your juice fasting journey and know that this will be an experience that will teach you and grow you into a better version of yourself.

JUICER IN THE SPOTLIGHT

Israel Torres, who has lost over 100 pounds during four 60-day juice fasts in 2012 and is a health champion now.

"I stumbled upon juicing during an office bet to lose weight and it was the best thing that could have happened to me *ever*. Green juicing is not only rebooting my body but also restoring the 20+ years of abuse I've put it through. I really wish I had learned about this sooner; however I now wake up everyday refreshed and amazed! There is logically nothing better that you can be putting in your body. I certainly feel we are at the advent of using secrets that have been dormant for thousands of years in today's mainstream world—it is just in time as obesity has become the number one killer."

Conclusion

Health is the greatest possession. Contentment is the great-est treasure. Confidence is the greatest friend.
~ Lao Tzu

Ever since I discovered and fell in love with juicing, I feel differently about fruits and vegetables. It's like really seeing something that was always there for the very first time. When was the last time you felt excited about fruits and vegetables in your super market aisle? I used to think of my produce as sustenance. Now I see it as a world of endless possibilities to play with and a gateway that brings me closer to Mother Nature. Even today, I still find new produce on the market that I haven't had before and immediately look it up to learn about its nutritional benefits and wonder if I can juice it. Even now as I sit here and think about my juicer, it fills me with anticipation on the next delicious batch I will be making. It cannot be soon enough!

I love this brave new world even five years later. I was walking down the aisle of my local Whole Foods store the other day and saying the names of every fruit and vegetable and every herb and plant in sight. There were a few exotic root vegetables and a couple of tropical fruits that I wasn't intimately familiar with . . . yet, but otherwise, I could give any new shopper of that produce section a thoroughly informative and fun tour around each fruit and vegetable!

Whether you are brand new to juicing or have been at this wonderful habit for a while, I am willing to bet your amazing juicing days are way ahead of you, yet to be had. The longer you stick with it, the better it gets. It's like wine, only much better for you and much easier to make at your home!

Let juicing be your one true present for yourself starting today. You probably don't need another sweater or pair of shoes or another electronic gadget, but what about a fantastic digestive and immune system, what about heaps of energy to last you all day long, what about more focus and awareness as you go through your beautiful life?

Juicing is a gift that keeps giving and a lifestyle that can enrich your existing one. Invest in a good juicer. Invest the time and effort to make your juices and invest in building a healthy strong body. Invest in you! Years from now, you won't regret that you didn't shop more or socialize more or work more, you may however regret that you didn't take better care of yourself . . . so start now. Juice, baby, juice! Don't give that regret a chance; instead, build your life with the powerful habit of juicing.

I know that juicing can become your best companion on a life-long journey to health and vitality. Just remember to not take yourself too seriously. Get high on juice, vitality and love of life. Have fun with it, make it exciting and weave it into your life with fierce love, compassion, persistence and joy. Let it be a glorious sunrise into a new way of living for you!

Ingredients and Highlights Index

shopping tips for, 86

grape

cleaning and storing, 116

mixing guidelines for, 212

recipes with, 143, 144

grapefruit

cleaning and storing, 115

mixing guidelines for, 211, 212

recipes with, 135, 149

rinds of, 94

H

herbs

cleaning and storing, 116

darlings, 106

fridge life, 81

list of for juicing, 99

most common, 208

honeydew

mixing guidelines for, 211

as replacement in recipes, 137

rinds of, 94–95

J

jalapeño pepper

benefits of, 207

mixing guidelines for, 212

as optional addition in recipes, 150, 172

recipes with, 145, 163

as replacement in recipes, 167

journal

digital, 235

for the experience, 235–236

for remembering recipes and results, 236–239

juice fasting

benefits of, 248–250

breaking the fast, 272–275

downsides of, 252–253

guidelines on length, 255–257

preparation for, 244–247, 260–262

juicing habit

motivation for, 217–219

overcome resistance of, 222–227

resistance of, 219–222

juice storage

cabbage, 178–179

how to, 177–178

how long, 177–178

juicer

how to choose, 69–72, 76–78

centrifugal

benefits, 72

downsides, 72

masticating

benefits, 73

downsides, 73

K

kale

cleaning and storing, 113

benefits of, 105

as replacement in recipes, 144, 145, 148, 161

recipes with, 141, 142, 143, 147, 164, 166, 168, 172, 190

shopping tips for, 80, 85

kiwi

recipes with, 137, 146

L

lemon

benefits of, 103

cleaning and storing, 115

mixing guidelines, 212

as optional addition in recipes, 136

recipes with, 135, 138, 142, 143, 148, 154, 155, 158, 161, 162, 164, 166, 191, 192

as replacement in recipes, 137, 139, 142, 151, 159

rind of, 94

lettuce

as replacement in recipes, 157, 168

Recipe Index